DOING THE DEED:

The Mechanics of
21st CENTURY PREACHING

Martha J. Simmons

Doing the Deed: The Mechanics of 21st Century Preaching
© 2012 by Martha J. Simmons
All rights reserved.

Published 2012 by
The African American Pulpit, Inc.
450 Piedmont Avenue, Atlanta, GA

Printed in the United States of America.

Library of Congress Cataloging-in-Publication Data is on file at the Library of Congress, Washington, D.C.

Simmons, Martha Jean
Doing the Deed: The Mechanics of 21st Century Preaching / Martha J. Simmons.
p. cm.

ISBN 978-0-9856426-1-7 (pbk: alk. paper)

Printed by Manuscript Management Group Inc.

Unless otherwise noted, the Scripture quotations in this publication are from the New Revised Standard Version of the Bible, copyright © 1989 by the Division of Christian Education of the National Council of Churches of Christ in the U.S.A. and used by permission.

DEDICATION

This study guide is dedicated to all preachers of the gospel, past, present, and future; to all of those in pews, pulpits, classrooms, and those in places and spaces too numerous to name who taught me to love God, the folk, and preaching; to all of those who, without formal training pierced skies and opened to me and the world the artistry of African American preaching; and to my mother, Mary, my many comrades in ministry, and all who love proclamation—thank you for being my guides on the journey of life.

CONTENTS

INTRODUCTION

In 1993, I co-authored and self-published a preaching study guide with Dr. Henry H. Mitchell. It was largely a companion to his book *Celebration and Experience in Preaching*. A very limited amount of what was said in that study guide is repeated here, because it bears repeating. Some of the mechanics of preaching are still the same; however, the ways in which some of them are utilized have changed, and those changes will be discussed. This time the aim is solely to provide as many preachers as possible with as many tools as possible for sermon preparation.

Although the book admittedly has leanings toward my faith community—the Protestant African American community—because so few books on the mechanics of preaching have been written with it in mind, the mechanics of preaching discussed in this book apply to all preachers, regardless of ethnicity. It's simply a matter of applying them to fit one's context. This study guide is also offered for use in the classroom, by pastors to train their preachers, and for **all** who desire to strengthen their preaching skills.

By the time you finish reading this study guide with its page after page of directions, recommendations, and exercises, you may believe that there is an avalanche of work that must be done to prepare a good sermon. You are right! There are no shortcuts if you want to produce good and great sermons. Thank goodness that the preparation process speeds up if you are committed to following the steps until you have learned each of them. After a while, the steps will be second nature for you. Also, keep in mind what you already know and do well. You can strengthen those areas last and tackle your problem areas first.

Additionally, keep in mind that your preaching aptitude and style will and SHOULD change over time. Your preaching should not sound the same at 60 as it did at 50, 40, 30, or 20. So, while you will know more as you go, there will be more to learn. That is the nature of preaching; it evolves and hopefully you will embrace the evolution and submerse yourself lifelong in the homiletics laboratory. Welcome to more lessons.

This study guide uses *vehicles*, which follow many of the chapters. I chose the term vehicle to mean that which carries us from one place or state of being to another. I determined from the previous study guide that these were helpful in enabling readers to become comfortable with principles of sermon design.

WHAT'S IN THIS STUDY GUIDE?

Chapter 1: Preaching at the Dawn of the 21st Century offers insights into some of the ways in which preaching has changed in the past 25 to 30 years, particularly in the African American faith community.

Chapter 2: Encountering the Whole Person addresses how preachers can avoid abstract preaching that leads to cognitive but not holistic, emotional (heart) assent to biblical messages. There are numerous ways to appeal to all of the senses of listeners. This chapter shows preachers how to do that.

Chapter 3: Artful Oratory: Making a Sermon Come Alive is concerned with various ways that preachers can produce vivid sermons. Preachers are taught how to find and use images in everything from books, to films, to videos and movies.

Chapter 4: Genres: Why Preachers Need to Understand Them is a type of literary structure and analysis primer for sermon development. Preachers can learn how to spot types of texts (stream of consciousness, narratives, parables, dialogues, group studies, poetry, etc.) found in the bible.

Chapter 5: Exegesis: What Does the Text Say and Mean? This the longest chapter in this study guide. It includes a discussion of lectionary preaching, text selection, asking the right questions of texts, historical analysis, and literary analysis.

Chapter 6: Focus. Focus. Focus. addresses what remains the most difficult problem of preachers—focusing a sermon. A step-by-step process is provided to help preachers stay focused through each paragraph of a sermon.

Chapter 7: The Art of Developing Titles, Introductions, Balance, Timing and Impact, and More concerns just what the chapter title indicates. Preachers are taught the art of developing titles, sermon introductions, how to make sure that a sermon is balanced, how to ensure that one's timing is not off during the preaching moment, and how to give attention to other small, but not unimportant, matters when constructing a sermon.

Chapter 8: Inclusive Preaching: Reaching All addresses thorny issues to which preachers must be attentive if they want to include and reach the marginalized and the outcast. Use of gender-inclusive language and ways to help preachers and churches stretch their boundaries of inclusiveness also are covered.

Chapter 9: Sermon Celebrations and Sermon Conclusions primarily focuses on how to conclude a sermon well, knowing when and how to do so in a celebratory fashion, and when to conclude with a challenge.

Chapter 10: Summing It All Up is the final chapter. It provides comments on previous chapters and a sermon as an example of all the principles taught in this study guide. The sermon is followed by note pages. These are provided to allow preachers to make notes related to each chapter in the study guide.

Now, on to preaching at the dawn of the 21st century.

1

PREACHING AT THE DAWN
OF THE 21ST CENTURY

Although every preacher certainly needs a thorough knowledge and cogent understanding of preaching theory (and texts used in seminaries provide this), too little is taught and written about the mechanics of preaching—how one does the deed. There is particularly a lack of information on the mechanics of preaching for the African American context.

Having studied preaching for one reason or another almost week in and week out for the past 16 years, and having preached almost twice that long, it is clear to me that some of the mechanics of preaching (particularly in African American contexts) have changed in the past 25 or so years. To know this, you have only to listen to sermons by premiere practitioners prior to 1980 and to the premier practitioners of the first decade of the 21st century.

THE BIG THEMES

A change has clearly occurred in the use of the BIG biblical/theological preaching themes. If a preacher wants to deliver a message that has weight or heft, he or she must begin with a BIG theme. This is not the same as starting with a short-list of Christian convictions that one has been taught over the years; and, then, looking for one of those principles in every passage one reads. No, the BIG themes are already there in the Word of God, in rituals, creeds, and in some of the songs of our faith. We just have to slowly, deliberately, and prayerfully read the bible and other documents and the BIG themes will clearly announce themselves.

Today's preaching, as compared to preaching of the past, is filled with fewer of the BIG themes (love, grace, justice, faith, forgiveness, discipleship, evil, creation, hospitality, hope, providence, sanctification, stewardship, suffering, and sin—just to name a few of the BIG themes). If the BIG themes are used, quite often they are watered down or cheapened. When they are watered down, it leads to a watering down of preaching, whether it is the topical preaching one is apt to do at Easter, Christmas, or Thanksgiving; or when the focus is on personal concerns such as grief, illness, loneliness, marriage, divorce, mental illness, etc.; or when one is addressing behaviors such as shame, jealousy, depression, or fear; or when one is preaching on pastoral themes.

Preachers should always avoid watering down their preaching. Today, providence is still used as a theme, but it is often watered down. As a BIG theme, providence can be summed up as: The Lord will make a way somehow, because *"all things work together for good for those who love God and are called according to the purposes of God"* (Romans 8:28). When watered down, providence, as a theme, can be summed up as:

God will work things out for us, because it is our season of blessing; or, because as children of God, we are entitled to be blessed.

We still hear grace used as a theme. However, too often, the grace preached is so "cheap" that at its foundation it is all crowns and no crosses, or all mercy and no personal responsibility.

Some of the current, favorite themes are prosperity, favor, and worship. Before a major recession hit the United States in 2008, almost every time we turned on the television or went to the Web to view a church service, we could be assured that at some point in the sermon we would hear preachers offer listeners prosperity or favor or admonish listeners to be greater worshipers. While focus on two of these themes (prosperity and favor) waned during the height of the recession (2008–2010), because so many were not prosperous and did not see evidence of the financial favor they had been promised, these themes did not die. Since such themes are easy to feed to the desperate and gullible, and fill coffers of preachers, it is likely that they will return in full force as the American economy stabilizes for larger numbers of people.

The use of worship as an often used preaching theme coincides with the advent of the acceptance of more demonstrative, and what some have called Pentecostal or Neo-Pentecostal-flavored church services, in non-Holiness and Pentecostal faith communities. In such services, parishioners are expected to clap their hands, raise their hands, shout, and do whatever can clearly be termed demonstrative worship. They may be asked to give God 30 or 60 seconds of praise, to open their mouths and praise God, or to pray out loud for the person next to them. The typical expectation with the latter request is that both the person praying and the one being prayed for will end up exhibiting demonstrative praise.

One can certainly not find fault with sincere demonstrative worship, if that is your cup of tea. My preference is for demonstrative, sincere worship. The problem is that typically congregations are only pointed toward one side of the worship coin—the side that makes for more energetic and louder responses. In the Hebrew language, if one engages in worship by prostrating himself or herself, the term used would be *"cagad."* This type of worship is promoted modernly. But, the other side of the worship coin is missing. This is the side that concerns *"latreia,"* a Greek word which defines worship as sacrifice and service for God, according to Levitical Law. Although we are no longer under the Law, complete and true worship still has two sides. One side points us toward God, and the other toward service to humanity. We rarely hear on television, and read on the Web and in books, sermons that discuss worship as service to others. Hearers need a balanced Word and worship experience led by those who proclaim the Word of God. It is fine to encourage demonstrative worship; however, it must be done in balance with encouraging people to serve others, thereby serving/worshiping God.

Be clear that most churches have never fed parishioners a steady diet of sermons using BIG themes such as justice and hospitality; and, in the Post-Modern era, less has been said about sin. All three themes were seen, more or less often, in the 1800s and 1900s, depending upon the social conditions of an era. However, the BIG themes are not relics of a by-gone era! They will always lead to weightier, more robust preaching, and, similarly, to Christian believers whose service to God is likewise.

Further, it is clear that those who do not constantly read and have knowledge of the BIG biblical/ theological themes and corresponding issues of their day will not be able to give more than surface treatment to either. Reading is still fundamental for good preaching. All else that is mentioned in this book will do little to serve the preacher who is not a regular reader of **more** than entertainment books, preaching magazines, preaching websites, the latest best-selling self-help books, and dumbed-down books and articles on everything from war to evolution.

Portability and Fitting Sermons

Before leaving this topic, let me offer brief words on two connected issues—portability and sermons that are fitting. Sermons that address subjects of little importance are also less portable. By portable, I mean the ability of a sermon to operate effectively in most venues where the Word of God is proclaimed. Not even the best preaching will gain a hearing in a mausoleum, which, unfortunately, describes the lack of spiritual vitality of a large number of churches around the world. These churches are not interested in preaching or even God for that matter. Their doors remain open for a variety of reasons, none of which have to do with Church business, the Sacraments of the Church, the purposes of the Church, or the spiritual needs of people. But, these are not the churches being discussed here.

The BIG themes of our faith community are big not only, but precisely, because they are the issues that concern all of humanity, even if they are not issues about which all of humanity is concerned. Sermons that concern small issues are insular in their focus and are less portable.

Directly related to portability is the issue of whether a sermon is "fitting," to use Fred Craddock's term. By fitting, I mean whether the Word of the Lord is the right word, in the right form and style, for a particular people at a particular point in history. More will be said about portability and how to prepare sermons that are fitting. But, both are raised here to buttress the argument for preaching that is focused on the BIG themes and issues of the Christian faith community.

STILL THE MAIN PROBLEM FOR ALL PREACHERS

While some things have changed relative to the mechanics of preaching, the inability of preachers to write and deliver focused messages continues as their main problem. This problem cuts across racial lines, genders, and age groups. All who teach preaching see it year in and year out. In one sermon after another, we have preachers mounting their sermonic horses and riding in all directions. Preachers still fail to focus sermons, and many take listeners around the world and back, to give a point that was just around the corner.

In a well-focused sermon, listeners can see the use of the text throughout the message, including at the conclusion. When a focused sermon is given, listeners also will be able to easily identify the aim of the sermon and how it applies to them and their actions. In other words, they will clearly know what the preacher hopes to have happen after the sermon is preached.

Contrastingly, a lack of focus causes preachers (especially those who preach sermons that are more than 25 minutes in length) to be repetitive and make the **same** point two or three different ways in the same sermon.

For African Americans, long sermons were more acceptable (though not necessarily a good idea), when all the congregation had to do the next day was go back to various types of drudgery or oppression. But, now that people know that one does not have to be long-winded to deliver a great message, and since listeners have family matters to which to attend, voice-mails and texts to answer, a week of meetings for which to prepare, social engagements, and more, they are less accepting of long sermons.

Throughout my life, there have been preachers to whom I could listen for more than 40 minutes. However, the list has always been short! Although it has been my experience that congregations will give a preacher a chance to pull together his or her sermonic thoughts while preaching, they will tolerate only so much scattered, poorly focused, long-winded preaching.

There is no shortcut to focused preaching. Most good preachers are focused writers even if they do not enter the pulpit with a manuscript. If a preacher's sermons are continually unfocused, the problem likely rests with his or her inability to write well and with other problems.

First, the writing problem. All of my peers who teach in seminaries have bemoaned the horrible writing of their students. They are clear that if they were to fail students for poorly written sermons or papers, they would typically flunk large segments of all of their classes!

As I write this study guide, I am mentoring four M.Div. students, two Ph.D. students, and four new pastors (at their churches less than four years). In all but one case, I have had to address their need to improve their writing. In two cases, I even mailed preachers copies of *The Scott, Foresman Handbook for Writers!* These are all bright and capable preachers, who either attended or are attending highly-ranked schools. However, most of these preachers were victims of elementary school level and high school educational systems that did not teach them to write well. And, after that, their bad writing was ignored, even in college and seminary!

If one cannot clearly state and cogently discuss a thesis in a term paper, the same problem will likely come through in his or her sermon writing and preaching. I have always firmly advocated that preachers take writing classes, even while they are working on M.Divs, D.Mins, and Ph.Ds. Sadly, good writing is not common in our society; and, with the advent of certain technological inventions, good writing is becoming less common each year. However, even those with writing problems would lose focus a lot less often if they were to keep their sermons short.

The second thing that often leads to a lack of sermonic focus is a lack of clarity in developing the behavioral focus of a sermon. The behavioral focus is similar in some ways to what Henry H. Mitchell refers to as the "behavioral purpose." For Mitchell, the behavioral purpose is the hook on which one hangs a sermon. The entire sermon is structured according to the behavioral purpose that a preacher determines. According to Mitchell, the behavioral purpose asks, "What do I want hearers to **do** after having heard a sermon?" A behavioral purpose accompanies each sermon and is not written in cognitive or negative terms, as it seeks to positively impact behavior. **It requires an inductive, not a deductive, approach to preaching.**[1] Instead of the term behavioral purpose, I prefer the term behavioral *focus*.

Every sermon should aim toward changed behavior! However, **I am convinced more than ever that to reach hearers emotionally and cognitively preachers need to begin by determining a behaviorally focused homiletical aim rooted in mutuality and solidarity,** about which I will say more shortly. This is more than determining a behavioral purpose, and it is more than making a claim upon the person preparing the sermon and the listeners, which is what homiletician Thomas Long recommends. It also requires an inductive approach.

The term "proposition" is also used by preachers to determine their sermon aim, though it may not necessarily be a behavioral aim. Homiletically speaking, the term as used by many African American preachers, comes from the late Dr. Samuel DeWitt Proctor. In *The Certain Sound of the Trumpet: Crafting a Sermon of Authority*, Proctor defines what he means by the term proposition, which he occasionally also refers to as the "thesis":

> The proposition is the one idea that has possessed the mind and stirred the soul of the preacher....
> It is a one-sentence statement that embraces a salient truth for the audience at that time....
> The proposition is a faith statement.... It means, this is what I shall have said when I am finished....

It is a contract that the preacher lays to the side of the desk to follow. . . . It is a sample of the preacher's total theology. . . . It is always a positive, affirmative, statement. . . .[2]

Another phrase used for much the same purpose as Proctor uses proposition is Haddon Robinson's "Big Idea." By it, he means "a central unifying idea must be at the heart of an effective sermon."[3] The Big Idea asks, "What is the preacher talking about and what is the preacher saying about what he or she is talking about?" Meaning, you have a subject or idea; now, what is its complement? Fusing the right subject with the right complement will get you to your Big Idea. The idea is then applied so that it is text-centered and audience-focused. Then the sermon is developed with examples and illustrations. It is applied, proved, or explained, for development, and constantly re-iterated (repeated) for force.[4]

As preachers design sermons, Tom Long offers that they should determine "the claim of the text upon the hearers and the preacher"; after the exegetical process, one is ready to create the sermon when he or she can finish the sentence: "in relation to those who will hear the sermon, what this text wants to say and do is. . ."[5] The claim of the text is occasion specific; it is what we hear on this day, from this text, for these people, in these circumstances at this juncture in their lives.[6] Further, "what the sermon aims to say can be called its focus, and what the sermon aims to do can be called its function." The focus and function statement should grow directly from the exegesis of the biblical text.[7] Long is definitely not advancing the sermonic form of a thesis and three points. Modernly, preachers are using a variety of methods (especially those just named above) to focus their sermons toward their desired aim.

Focus problems also occur as a result of preachers who are ambivalent about sermons they prepare. This can be especially difficult for those who often preach from lectionaries, but may be in contexts that are far different for those who select the lectionary texts each year. Context matters and one's preaching equilibrium can be clearly thrown off balance or one can become homiletically fatigued if too often a preacher is faced with texts that he or she has to struggle to make fit his or her context.

In a similar vein, less focus is likely if one preaches about themes about which she or he is not invested. Every preacher of some seniority has a story about an annual day or sermon theme they dreaded preaching and about lectionary passages that bored them to tears or which they felt offered little of what their congregation needed at a given moment.

INDIVIDUALISM

As preaching topics such as "Prosperity" and "Cheap Grace" have risen (some would say, again) in popularity, alongside them an increase in individualistic preaching, as opposed to communal preaching, also has risen. Communal preaching is concerned with the well-being of communities. Communities include individuals, families, and the whole of society.

Communal preaching is particularly important for communities that are faced with serious, death-promoting issues, day after day and decade after decade. Communal preaching does not hide behind church doors or doctrines of separatism, nor does it push people to become insular and selfish. It embraces a gospel that is servant-minded and seeks the welfare of communities and countries and operates to create believers who do the same.

Today, people are not apt to attend the churches their parents and grandparents attended, if their parents and grandparents attended church at all. So, one of the foundations for communal preaching—generations of blood-kin believers—is weakened. Also, the generation gap in churches is clearer. Many pastors now speak of pastoring four or five generations in one church. One wonders how well preachers are handling the balancing act of preaching to four or five generations in one church. Yes, we've always had four and five generations in our churches; it's just that now individuals are more adamant and honest about wanting a Word that speaks to their specific generation.

Additionally, Americans increasingly are not biblically literate or generally literate about religion, as one study after another (especially those by Pew and The Hartford Institute for Religion Research) continues to show. Further, preachers are no longer the end-all and be-all for biblical and religious knowledge. Those who are able to do so can now read the Scriptures through a variety of sources. They can make their own decisions about the Scriptures, and they have a great deal of material to aid in their quest for biblical understanding. I am not recommending this as the best practice for study of the Word, as it is a practice that lessens community; I am just stating that it is a reality.

Moreover, now, far too often, people are not mainly interested in what they can do for their community or the world. Individualism has become strongly embedded in the psyche of the individual, country, and the Church. Listeners are interested in what the message can allow *them* to do for *themselves and their kind and kin.* How can they expand *their* territory, get *their* break-through, have *their* season of harvest, feed *their* family, send *their* children to college, and build a great life for *themselves*?

Then, there is the snookering of believers by prosperity gospel preaching which promotes individualism. Unfortunately, this type of preaching has also filled stadiums and gained television notoriety for numerous preachers. It shows no signs of abating. And, it is popular to many young preachers, and to some who have struggled in congregations with scarce resources for many years, as a silver bullet, that they hope will fill seats and offering plates.

Additionally, since preaching does not operate in a cultural vacuum, we cannot forget the rise in individualism that always rears its head in the Church whenever the political parties and controllers of financial systems (gas/oil, financial systems, media empires, etc.) weigh in to widen the cultural and economic divide, when it serves them. Michael Jinkins wrote in a 2012 blog about some of the variants of individualism and how they play out, especially when stoked by politicians and financial systems. Here are four according to Jinkins:

(1) Individuals have priority over community, and the only right that ultimately counts for anything is the right of the individual not to be constrained by the needs or interests of others.

(2) Altruism is suspect because the only thing we can vouch for with anything approaching certainty is the purity of self-interest and the will to survive.

(3) The single great power we can trust is the power of the economic free market to reward industry and provide the greatest good.

(4) The middle way, moderation, negotiation and compromise are evils because morality has no shades of gray.[8]

All of this helps make the atmosphere ripe for individualistic or non-communally focused preaching. Remember, most of the texts of the bible were written to a faith **community**. David Buttrick says:

Even when texts are ostensibly addressed to individuals—"Theophilus" (Luke 1:3), "Philemon" (Philem. 1), . . .—they are nonetheless addressed to individuals who share communal Christian consciousness. Thus, texts do not address individuals in individual self-awareness. . . . Therefore as interpreters we do not ask "What does the text say to me?". . . . but "What is the text saying to our faith-consciousness?" . . . The real problem with much therapeutic preaching today is not that it is therapeutic, for after all various therapies have helped us all, but that it turns communal language into language addressing an individual in self-awareness.[9]

One of the pericopes that has become a staple in this season of rugged individualistic preaching is the story of Joseph in Genesis. Just do a quick check of the number of sermons concerning Joseph preached by African American clergy between 1999 and 2010, and you will find that they proliferate the preaching landscape. I first noticed this in sermons that were submitted to *The African American Pulpit Journal* for the same period, and then checked other sources to see if this was being done elsewhere by African American preachers. And, indeed it was! To see that the same thing was done by non-African American clergy during the same period, all one has to do is Google the phrase "sermons using the biblical story of Joseph," and go to the non-African American websites.

Why? Here's my theory. With the return of the Prosperity Gospel to mass audiences through a variety of media, the story of Joseph—a story about a man whose actions reunite his family and save a nation—has become a story about **one** man's setbacks that were just setups for **his** comeback. The Joseph story, as it is typically modernly preached, only mentions his family as one of his setbacks, not his primary concern. Such preaching of this story purposely "turns communal language into language addressing an individual in **self-awareness**." This text is the perfect 21st-century tool for preachers to esigete, as they seek to offer therapeutic, individualistically focused messages.

First, it is easy to follow. The story is written in narrative form, which is a common genre for preaching and one to which everyone can relate. We all love a good story with a few plot twists and a happy ending. Second, the story concerns issues with which everyone is familiar: sibling rivalry; being lied upon; doing a good deed that is forgotten; moving up the ladder of success in spite of going through a great deal of difficulty as you climb; achieving a highly honored position; having one's siblings have to depend on you after they have mistreated you; bringing a family together; and more. Third, the story offers people a winning outcome against overwhelming odds and constant setbacks. Surely, this is the type of story those facing oppressive and confusing life circumstances want to hear. Fourth, it allows for the constant demonization of others—those who tried to stop Joseph from being successful, and those who try to stop those to whom his story is preached. In this approach to the story, little or nothing is said about Joseph's responsibility for any of his difficulties. And, fifth, since the story has been used by so many preachers who are well-known and wealthy, it suggests to those preachers who follow these preachers and want to be like them that they should use it in the same way; and, they have.

BEHAVIORALLY FOCUSED SERMONS GROUNDED IN MUTUALITY AND SOLIDARITY

Perhaps as another vestige of this country's focus on individualism, preachers continue to approach sermon preparation without a behavioral bottom-line and with a lone-ranger approach. Christine Smith wrote almost 25 years ago in her book *Weaving the Sermon*:

> [There is a type of preaching that] supports the dichotomy of preacher and community as separate and distinct realities. The questions would be very different if they [sermons] were designed to help a preacher construct a sermon event or a moment of proclamation that was rooted in solidarity.

They might then read: In this moment of faith sharing, what are we trying to explore, create or articulate together? What can we all see together in these moments of proclamation? What do you illumine for me in terms of mystery and faith, what do I illumine for you, and what truths can we bring to light together? What are our hopes as a community for these shared moments together? What do we hope will happen?

These very different guiding questions, if used to shape our preaching, will root the process of proclamation much more deeply in creating mutuality and solidarity.[10]

. . . . It is not talking about solidarity; it is about creating it by the very act of proclamation. Preaching from a feminist perspective asserts that greatest mutuality is achieved and experienced among equals. Thus, in preaching, the truths of the entire community need to be honored, expressed and sought out if true mutuality is at the heart of faith sharing.[11]

After decades of hearing sermons, writing sermons, reading sermons, preaching sermons, grading sermons, editing sermons, wrestling with sermons, loving sermons, hating sermons, being blessed by sermons, being angered by sermons, and being convicted by sermons, I believe the greater part of designing a well-written sermon is ensuring that it is behaviorally focused and grounded in mutuality and solidarity. Gone should be the days when preachers prepare sermons without totally understanding that they do so within a community, not in isolation, as oracles summoned from on high to tell people what they need to hear. Too much of the notion of prophets standing on sacred islands alone, as God delivers unto them gospel pearls for the people, remains in the pulpit.

In the case of the African American community, so much weight was placed on the shoulders of its early preachers. Their sermons and their lives had to fight slave masters and encourage people to remain hopeful while living through daily drudgery and daily hell. They had to stand as the village teachers, even if they could not read or write. They were father figures (and a few females who dared to preach in the 1700s and 1800s) to a community where consistent genealogical fatherhood was not even allowed. In many instances, they were the only voices in the entire community given a modicum of respect; and, at least in the Church, though often under threat of death, they could critique the slavery-monetary-driven status quo system and birth in listeners the courage to do the same.

W. E. B. Du Bois spoke of the African American preacher in his treatise, *The Souls of Black Folk*, when he wrote: "The preacher is the most unique personality developed by the Negro on American soil."[12] Another scholar wrote:

Upon examination of the listed ways in which the African American pastor constructs communities of influence—civil rights activities, ministerial alliances, operation of child care centers, surrogate father in households headed by single mothers, and family arbitrators, just to name a few—one will find that the role of the African American pastor of today is a continuation of the historic role assigned to them by the church and the community.[13]

So, it is no wonder that from these beginnings, future generations of preachers would come to see themselves and be seen as centers of proclamation. However, this was never the total picture. It is simply a matter of how history is written. The leaders always get the majority of the credit and often have their roles made larger-than-life, especially in a society focused on rugged individualism rather than a village model. The fact is, whether in the white or the black community, or a community of any ethnicity, when it comes to the work of the Church, it is always the congregation that is doing the lion's share of the building, the burden bearing, and the leading. It has always been the women, the deacons, the prayer warriors, the mission sisters, etc. (some of whom were lay preachers) who often led worship. Remember, from the mid-1700s to the mid-1900s, there was not a sufficient number of preachers or pastors to serve all of the people who gathered in storefronts and churches around the country. Lay people often kept these churches going.

So, once and for all, let us put to rest this notion of the lone-ranger preacher preparing a sermon to be delivered **to** the people. Instead, during sermon preparation, let us shift toward behaviorally focused preaching that is grounded in solidarity and mutuality. This will aid in less preacher worship, televangelist superstar worship, and the faithful looking to preachers **only** for what "thus saith the Lord."

Lord, deliver us from sermons designed to build group think, according to any preacher's design. Deliver us from churches where there is only *one* resident theologian, and deliver us from placing an unnecessary and historically incorrectly written-about burden upon preachers, and they upon themselves. Indeed, we need mutuality and solidarity between preachers and congregations and sermons designed in this vein.

PREACHER-DRIVEN CALL-AND-RESPONSE

Call-and-response that is cooperative and communal is a hallmark of the African American faith community. In this arrangement, neither the preacher nor the congregation is the leader. Instead, the Spirit blows where it will and all are blessed by the mutually consuming warmth of the Holy Ghost. This has been widely written about.

Currently, if one were to visit a vibrant and high-energy African American church, particularly those with pastors under age 55, they would likely hear the use of a string of urgings **from the preacher** during the sermon. Commonly used urgings include: "Tell your neighbor…."; "Give the Lord either a hand-clap of praise or some praise"; "Touch two people and say…."; and say thus and so—"Say favor," "Say blessed," "Say, I'm going higher," and you get the idea. Done in this same vein, other calls by preachers for responses include phrases such as: "You missed it," "This will shout you," and "You missed your shout cue."

There are still call-and-response moments that are cooperative, even in the former churches. However, when not in response to the preacher's urging, other than an occasional heartfelt "Amen," these calls and responses from the congregation are often calls for help for the preacher—"Lord, help"; "Hold on, Preacher"; and "Pray church." The amount of cooperative call-and-response has greatly decreased in these settings. Once upon a time, one had to earn, by preaching well or poorly (thus receiving congregational pleas for one's rescue), a call-and/or-response from the congregation.

Not so with preacher-driven call-and-response, which carries with it an air of entitlement. This rhetorical strategy was given broad usage and some would say credence, as it was used more frequently, beginning in the 1990s, by well-known African American televangelists and mega-church pastors and revivalists, and even some non-African American televangelists.

While it is not problematic for a preacher to encourage call-and-response, one has to wonder what the intent is behind a barrage of never-ending calls for responses by preachers during their sermons. Surely it is not to encourage unity. The church has historically been able to deliver unified calls-and-responses without much urging by preachers, except as such urging is done through the delivery of strong messages. Is it to heighten enthusiasm for the gospel? Perhaps. But doesn't good preaching and well-planned liturgy do that? Perhaps there are good reasons for excessive preacher-driven call-and-response. I just cannot name one.

So, I leave it up to each preacher to determine why they need to excessively and constantly place calls for responses in sermons.

One hopes that these calls are not being made just because it is something that's popular; or, because it is done by well-known and wealthy preachers; and/or, those on television. I also hope that such calls are not beckonings designed to build group-think by preachers. By this I mean preachers excessively calling for responses in order to create a sense that the congregation is on one accord and agrees with what he or she (the preacher) is saying. In such circumstances, the preacher becomes pastor, lead liturgist, and the final word on the Word. What space is left for the Spirit, ushering all to lift their voices in communion as the Church as a chorus, giving sincere utterances to God?

THE IMPACT OF TECHNOLOGY

Sermons are now accompanied by sounds, images on screens, dance presentations, and whatever preachers can dream up. A sermon on love might begin with a CD playing Stevie Wonder's song "These Three Words" (and, of course, the three words are "I love you") in the background. A sermon on tithing may be accompanied by a buffet table of food, using the buffet as a metaphor for all bounty given by God, and dividing the food to show that we get to keep 90 percent of the food and that 10 percent of it is to go to God. Scriptures may appear on screens or are read by preachers from BlackBerries and i-Phones, and surely you've now seen sermons preached using iPads and other tablets.

Technology is being used to establish a worship mood that drapes the sanctuary before sermons begin. We now have churches with Drama and Arts Ministries. These ministries can fill the room with the agony of the crucifixion, bring to life the starkness of John the Baptist's life in the wilderness, or provide a view of the neighborhood of the woman at the well. They do it through large, sometimes almost life-like props in the pulpit and through the use of screens and graphics. If a preacher can think of it, technology can create it. This helps—but it can also hurt—preaching.

First, how it can hurt. Technology hurts when it becomes a crutch on which preachers lean to craft scenes and moods that they are unable to craft in their sermons, due to their limited vocabulary and limited homiletical imagination. Technology hurts when people are more focused on a picture, a scene, a mime enactment, or even a song than they are on the preaching of the Word that is meant to be brought to the fore by the songs, images, drama, and arts enactments or re-enactments. Technology hurts when it becomes the spectacle to which people are attracted, rather than the cross—wooden, bloodied, and on the third day, bare—or to the good news that came as a baby in a stable and comes among us again and again.

A few years ago, a well-known television preacher did a sermon series from the book of Revelation. Behind him, before and during the sermon, were things such as a very tall picture of some artist's rendition of how the 4 Horsemen of the Apocalypse should look, the beast of the sea with 7 heads and 10 horns, and an artistic depiction of a new heaven and a new earth. One could barely hear the preacher, for looking at the images—and I was watching on television. Imagine being present for these worship services! To this, he added gasps and other sounds to heighten the fear one should feel during the impending days of doom discussed in the book of Revelation. Perhaps the preacher thought this pageantry necessary to make his sermon series memorable and interesting.

Although I listened carefully to the sermons, because of research I was doing, I had no real memory of the content of the sermons just days later. However, the images are still embedded in my memory, mainly because I found so many of them over-the-top and factually questionable. If one puts himself or herself out as a user of props and images, great care must be taken to make sure that the scriptural exegesis and historical representations being presented are correct. Then, a way must be found to continually bring people back to the Word, not the props or images on a screen. The props and images must be submersed in the sermon in a way that allows them to exist in service of the Word, and not vice versa.

Preachers must also be careful of the ways they use images in a commodity-driven culture. We can become purveyors of the same tactics used by unscrupulous advertisers to sell products. Do not be naïve: mediums have an impact on our messages. And, if the main thing that we are selling is pomp, gimmicks, and props, what do people have when they leave?

Technology can also help make a good or great sermon more memorable. In this age of visual stimulation, preachers do not need to apologize for crafting worship to appeal to the visual senses. The best preachers have always used images, even if they only had words with which to paint. Now we can physically place images before hearers too.

Face it, we now live in an age where most people expect the use of technology during worship. This is the new normal. As Shane Hipps points out in one of his books on technology and the Church, there has been a dramatic shift in how people "experience the personal." So, embrace technology; but, be wise in its use. If your church can afford screens, do not minimize or waste their use by only placing songs and scriptures on them. Such use of screens reduces the overall sensory experience of people to the visual; and, we know that people are much more than what they can see.

Use screens to help set moods but not overpower worship. Use screens to help people remember the points/moves in sermons. On a recent occasion, when I served as a guest preacher, I preached in a church that had screens. My sermon was entitled "A Zig Zag Life"; the text was Exodus 13:17-18. Weeks before going to the church, I sent to the media staff on a travel-drive segments of the sermon and images that I wanted to appear on screen as I preached. For two segments of the sermon, it was my sense that if hearers saw relevant and colorful images zigging and zagging, that would make the entire sermon more memorable. After listening to the feedback of the pastor for whom I preached, and watching a video of the sermon, I believe it worked better than I could have imagined. I've also used persons to mime sections of sermons as I preached. Again, the result was the same.

Additionally, use screens and other media and images to do things such as: to remember and honor the lives of deceased members; to celebrate big events in the life of your church and in the life of the members; to increase the involvement of church members in community activities and issues; and to promote the ministries of your church that need uplift, typically missions, Christian education, evangelism, social justice, and children's ministries. All of this aids in the sermonic moment and in community building as a church comes together to be uplifted and lifted to a higher standard by the Holy Spirit and the Word of God.

Do not waste technology or become a slave to it. Find a balance. Two books that may aid in your use and more thorough understanding of the potential of technology and its impact on the Church are David Lochhead's, *Shifting Realities: Information Technology and the Church*; and, Shane Hipps's, *The Hidden Power of Electronic Culture: How Media Shapes Faith, the Gospel, and the Church*.

SPEED

Have you noticed how much faster many of today's preachers preach? Having worked in publishing for quite some time, I know that those who give voice to audio-books are recommended to speak 150–160 words per minute, which is the range that people comfortably hear and vocalize words. But, if you've listened carefully to numerous African American and non-African American clergy over the last 25 years, their speed is closer to 200 words per minute.

I began noticing the change in the speed of preaching in the late '80s. Certainly, several things account for the change in speed of much of today's African American preaching. However, hip hop culture, especially its music and approach to delivering the spoken word with rhythms and beats, provides one of the best vantage points by which we can understand the change in the speed of speech in African American and American culture.

In the 1980s, the quick rhythms, rhymes, and cadences of hip hop culture began firmly implanting themselves within mainstream African American culture and later in the wider American culture. It was typical to hear those who did not come of age during this period say, when listening to rap music: "I don't know what they said in that song. They said it too quickly." Hip hop lyrics were spoken quicker, and in some cases much quicker, than the songs that preceded them. Those who were comfortable and grew up with this change in speed, whether they knew it or not, transferred it throughout their lives, including into their preaching. Maybe it is incorrect to say that they transferred it, for they were familiar with little else. They were just speaking at a rate that felt natural. This was the pace at which they had come to understand and hear words.

Now, I just expect faster sermons (especially from preachers age 40ish and under). I believe that this pace of preaching is the new normal for many. What does this mean? Long-term, it is hard to say. Currently, it means that a slow, brooding Reverend Caesar Clark (deceased pastor of Good Street Baptist Church, Dallas, Texas) might appeal today to those of us who love good preaching at any speed; but, he would likely lose many of today's young adults and younger listeners after 10 or 15 minutes, because of his slow pace and his style that left his greatest emotional eruption for the end of the sermon.

I vividly recall, just seven years or so ago, listening to one of the greatest preachers in the English-speaking world (as determined by one magazine and decades of listings of this type) stand before a young adult audience, who cringed as he delivered one slow line after another and with numerous pauses. I knew what was happening and so did the pastor who held the guest preacher in high esteem too. A few days later, the pastor confided to me that the chair of his Young Adult Ministry (age 38) indicated that perhaps the preacher would have been better for Seniors Sunday. The pastor and I were clear that the guest preacher had delivered a sermon that was exegetically sound, that the subject was appropriate for the context, and that *we* were helped by the sermon and moved by the eloquent use of language by the preacher. But, we both also knew what was missing. The speed of the sermon was too slow and the energy level that accompanied the pace of the sermon was not high enough for youth and young adults. Since then, I've seen this happen again and again to older and younger preachers who spoke too slowly and with too little energy.

Whether we like it or not, the listening sensibilities of many in our churches have sped up. This means that, because sped-up speech done well acts as its own medium of emotionally charged speech, a preacher who is comfortable with speed, standing before those who have ears to hear, may be able to evoke as dramatic an impact as the slow old-school whooper (defined on page 16) does in many African American church contexts.

You only have to hear the preaching of Frederick Haynes III of Friendship West Church of Dallas or Lance Watson of St. Paul's Baptist Church of Richmond to prove the point. Neither is an old-school whooper, but their speed of speech produces such a powerfully rhythmic and emotionally charged experience that crowds are just as moved as if they were listening to whoopers. View portions of various sermons by either on YouTube or elsewhere to further understand what I mean.

FIRE OUT THE GATE THAT PERMEATES

Another change in 21st-century preaching can be identified by what I term *fire out the gate that permeates*. This means that early in the sermon the preacher has the congregation on its feet for one of several times. This fire (or high energy) is placed throughout the sermon and results in listeners standing in acknowledgment of things said by the preacher as many as five or six times before the conclusion of the message, and again at the conclusion of the message.

This preaching is energetic, and often those who do it are drenched with sweat by the mid-point of a message. Preachers who use the *fire out the gate that permeates* method also tend to involve their bodies frequently in preaching. They do not stand flat-footed and still. Throughout the sermon, their arms flail; they may jump, display various head movements, and the entire bodies of some even shake. All of this movement is in keeping with the high level of verbal and physical energy they bring to the preaching moment.

There is no way to tell how wide-spread this practice will become, nor exactly what caused its rise. However, it is clear that this method is now used by many of the best-known African American preachers, male and female, and numerous clergy of other ethnicities. Likely, television, streaming, and revival preaching have aided in the prominence of the *fire out the gate that permeates* method, as it has become common to see preachers in local and national broadcasts use it.

I am particularly intrigued by this method of preaching. Although I have only anecdotally studied this method, for a few years, some aspects of it are immediately attractive. First, it requires that one be especially attentive to each line of a sermon, as one determines points, stories, and illustrations that are likely to bring people out of their seats. Certainly, one should always be attentive to each line of a sermon, because they are handling the Word of God. However, this method of sermon writing almost provides an insurance card to ensure that this is done. The preacher is not out to perform or impress a congregation. He or she simply arranges the sermon in a particular way and is prepared to preach each section with the energy required to gain the desired response from a congregation. It is not easy to get listeners to stand to their feet again and again, Sunday after Sunday. Over time, those who preach this way arrange or prepare their sermons, in this fashion, without thinking about it. It becomes instinctual. One selects a BIG issue, designs the sermon for maximum impact, and delivers it with high energy.

Second, this type of preaching tends to value illustrations. These high-energy preachers know that illustrations greatly aid preaching, if they are not overused and are on-point.

Third, this style requires great use of one's body. I believe that, for too long, the body has been under-utilized in preaching, even in the African American Church, which is historically known for demonstrative preaching. Although extensive use of the body will certainly not suit every preacher, increased use of the body by those who tend to stand flat-footed could do a great deal to increase the energy level of their preaching. My sense is that most preachers want to offer sermons that are more, not less, energetic. Increased use of the body can help with this.

Fourth, this type of preaching is attractive because it requires continuous energy, and a great deal of modern preaching lacks energy. This explains (in part) the decline in good preaching among so many white denominations and some black ones—preachers are not trained to deliver the Word with power and energy. If the aim is to ensure that people are on their feet at least four or five times before one reaches his or her conclusion in a 20 to 30 minute sermon, preachers will need to maintain a high level of energy throughout the sermon, rather than just at the end of the sermon, which is historically the peak of emotional release in African American preaching.

Please do not misunderstand me. The best preachers have historically offered sermons that were memorable throughout and at the end. However, it takes one type of preaching to make an entire message memorable and another to make it memorable **and** have people stand to their feet to acknowledge most of the memorable moments. Also, please be clear that having listeners on their feet four or five times during a sermon is not a preaching aim that is to be used as a gimmick or for personal aggrandizement. Instead, it is simply an energy gauge for writing and delivering a sermon. Finally, "fire out the gate" style preaching, as with all preaching, must be occasion appropriate. One may not want to use it during a funeral, wedding homily, or similar occasions. However, for those who view funerals as celebratory home-goings, it may work.

LESS MELODY IN AFRICAN AMERICAN PREACHING

Many of today's best African American preachers are not whoopers, as the term has been historically used and understood. This is not to say that the African American faith community does not still love whooping. Likely, the average African American preacher would still whoop, if he or she could. And, some of today's best-known preachers (E. Dewey Smith, Jasper Williams Jr., and Carolyn Knight of Atlanta, Ralph West of Dallas, Rudolph McKissick Jr. of Florida, and Paul Morton of Atlanta and New Orleans, etc.) still whoop. All of the African American preachers I have asked about whooping during my years in ministry (except one, who I believe was not being totally honest) have indicated that they would love to have it in their preaching arsenal, even if they only use it occasionally.

What is whooping? In *Preaching with Sacred Fire: African American Sermons, 1750 to the Present,* I wrote:

> In the introduction to *Sacred Symphony: The Chanted Sermon of the Black Preacher,* homiletician William Turner of Duke Divinity School writes: "That which is variously referred to as whooping, intoning, chanting, moaning or tuning is essentially melody. This particular style of melody is definable as a series of cohesive pitches which have continuity, tonality, quasi-metrical phraseology and formulary cadence."

> Whooping is first melody. It can be identified by the fact that its pitches are logically connected and have prescribed/punctuated rhythms, which require certain modulations of the voice, and is often delineated by quasi-metrical phrasings.

> Charles Adams . . . undoubtedly referring to pre-1970s styles, says of whooping: "That the line between singing and preaching is very thin is boldly illustrated in the Black American slave preacher's practice of a form of proclamation that transformed declarative and didactic speech into dramatic and celebratory song. That is what the Black preacher's vaunted whoop is all about."[14]

While whooping is still loved and admired in many quarters of the African American faith community, whooping with extensive melody (also known as old-school whooping) is not common among today's younger African American preachers, especially those who are seminary-trained. It has never been common among women, mainly because it was considered a manly art form; and, women had so few opportunities to see it modeled and to learn how to release it, even when it was shut up in their bones.

There are now fewer models from which this style of whooping can be learned by either men or women. Most of today's best-known African American clergy (especially those on national television) do not whoop, or do so only sporadically. Old-style whooping is also seen less because whooping has transitioned. On this point, I wrote in *Preaching with Sacred Fire*:

> The first noticeable transition that occurred in whooping in more than two hundred-plus years was marked by the preaching of Reverend Charles Gilchrest Adams. Although a preacher long before the 1970s, he became a revivalist and academic lecturer of national note in the late '70s. African American audiences knew that his preaching was different. It was filled with multiple alliterative lists; it was serious. It could contain four or five crescendo moments that are as high as the typical sermon celebration/conclusion of most whoopers, and it had cadence, but almost no melody. Listeners knew that it was not a typical form of whooping, but it resembled whooping, and connoisseurs of the art form knew that it was whooping. The Adams style of whooping was much more subtle than those who hacked or even the melodic whoopers but it was whooping. Because Adams was considered erudite (a Harvard graduate), he turned on their head all of the traditional notions of whoopers as persons with little formal education or substandard education. Nevertheless, listeners knew what he was doing was whooping, so he was dubbed the "Harvard whooper."

> As with Adams, some other preachers place tonality throughout the sermon. This is most often seen in the Church of God in Christ and other Holiness-Pentecostal faith communities. While this might seem to rob the sermon of high impact at conclusion, these whoopers see the sermon as a series of celebrations. For this type of preacher, all holy communication must be done in what is considered holy tone.

> However, this is not what Adams, or those whose preaching styles have evolved from his, does. While his preaching is filled with a great deal of cadence, one becomes aware that he is not constantly signaling a movement toward what W. E. B. Du Bois called "frenzy,"[15] more commonly known as shouting. Frenzy can break out at any time during the preaching of whoopers in certain faith communities. Adams instead moves through a sermon with cadence, only as a vehicle of modulation. His cadence helps him modulate his continuous production of long alliterative lists (also referred to as producing runs and riffs), which is a hallmark of his preaching. "Those who stand in the Adams lineage . . . also use cadence as a vehicle to modulate their production throughout the sermon."[16]

The post-1970s forms of whooping are much less melodic and filled with fewer pauses. They require a quick speech pace, and can contain numerous crescendos and continuous cadence.[17] This is good news for young preachers, especially African American female preachers. Although both would likely whoop, if they could, they know that the transition has occurred, so there is less pressure to try to learn this art form if one does not do it naturally.

SUMMATION

There is a need for the mechanics of preaching to be taught more in seminaries. Some of the mechanics of preaching have indeed changed in the past 25 years. Sermons now contain fewer of the BIG themes. Too much of preaching now concerns prosperity and only focuses on one aspect of worship. Cultural individualism has increased and its impact can be seen in modern preaching.

Focus remains a problem that plagues most preachers. Focus can be greatly aided if preachers design sermons so that they are behaviorally focused and grounded in solidarity and mutuality with congregations and communities.

Preaching is now driven less by cooperative call-and-response. Preachers need to determine why and if they need call-and-response that they lead.

Technology is now a mainstay in churches. It can help preaching, when it is not used as a crutch for preachers who use it instead of strong vocabularies and strong homiletical imaginations.

The speed of African American preaching and preaching by those in other ethnic communities is faster than in the past. There has been a rise in preaching that is fiery (energetic) at the beginning of sermons (fire out the gate), and this fire permeates entire messages.

Finally, whooping, long a crown jewel of African American preaching, also has transitioned. It now contains less melody. This is good news for young preachers, if they are not natural whoopers, and for African American female preachers who have never had enough role models to learn how to whoop well; and or were penalized for use of this art form in their preaching, because it has historically mainly been done by African American men.

With all of that said, I now move to ways that preachers can craft and deliver good sermons amid all of the changes that have occurred in the mechanics of preaching and in culture in the last 20 or so years.

NOTES

1. For a thoughtful analysis of the inductive verses deductive approach, see Fred Craddock's *As One without Authority: Essays on Inductive Preaching* (Enid, OK: Phillips University, 1971) and his *Overhearing the Gospel* (Nashville: Abingdon, 1978). Tom Long's *The Witness of Preaching* (Louisville: Westminster John Knox, 1999) adds to the discussion on the subject that was begun by Craddock and others.

2. Samuel Proctor, *The Certain Sound of the Trumpet: Crafting a Sermon of Authority* (Valley Forge, PA: Judson Press, 1994), 33–40.

3. Haddon Robinson, *Biblical Preaching: The Development and Delivery of Expository Messages,* 2nd Edition (Grand Rapids, MI: Baker Academic, 2001), 37.

4. Ibid., 39–47.

5. Thomas G. Long, *The Witness of Preaching,* 2nd Edition (Louisville: Westminster John Knox, 2005), 98.

6. Ibid., 100.

7. Ibid., 109.

8. Michael Jinkins, "Faith and Political Rhetoric," February 7, 2012, on the Call and Response blog of Duke Divinity School. Michael Jinkins is the president of Louisville Presbyterian Theological Seminary (accessed February 15, 2012).

9. David Buttrick, *Homiletic Moves and Structures* (Philadelphia, PA: Fortress Press, 1987), 277.

10. Christine Smith, *Weaving the Sermon* (Louisville, KY: Westminster/John Knox Press, 1989), 57.

11. Ibid., 56.

12. W. E. B. Du Bois, *The Souls of Black Folk* (New York, NY: W.W. Norton, 1999), 120–123.

13. James Jenkins, "The African American Baptist Pastor and Church Government: The Myth of the Dictator," *Journal for Baptist Theology and Ministry* 2.1 (2004): 74.

14. Martha Simmons and Frank Thomas, eds., *Preaching with Sacred Fire: African American Sermons, 1750 to the Present* (New York, NY: Norton Publishers, 2010), 865.

15. *The Souls of Black Folk,* 133.

16. *Preaching with Sacred Fire,* 874–875.

17. Ibid., 875.

2

ENCOUNTERING THE WHOLE PERSON

Before moving to the subject of holistic encounter, it is time to define terms that will be used throughout the remainder of this study guide.

Celebration—This term was firmly planted in homiletical literature by homiletician Henry H. Mitchell. By celebration, he means the conclusion of the sermon in a manner that allows for hearers to be glad about the sermon content they have experienced and the future that the content of the sermon portends, if hearers accept directions and encouragement given through the sermon. Frank A. Thomas, a student of Mitchell, defined celebration as "the culmination of the sermonic design, where a moment is created in which the remembrance of a redemptive past and/or the conviction of a liberated future transforms the events immediately experienced."[1]

Conclusion—The sermon conclusion is simply the end of the sermon. A conclusion may or may not be a celebration. A sermon may also conclude with a challenge. Ending a sermon with a challenge means that the preacher is directing or summoning listeners to engage or not engage in certain behavior.

Exegesis—For purposes of this study guide, the term exegesis is defined as the critical, historical interpretation or explication of biblical texts.

Hermeneutics—The art of interpretation which includes understanding the meaning, use, and construction of words and people. Preachers use their hermeneutical lens (their view of the world) as their interpretive framework in approaching texts.

Homiletics—The study of homilies or sermons.

Move—The term is credited to homiletician David Buttrick, who says, "In speaking of "moves," we are deliberately changing terminology. For years preachers have talked of making *points* in sermons. The word "point" is peculiar; it implies a rational, at-a-distance pointing at things, some kind of objectification.". . . Instead, we are going to speak of moves, of making moves in a movement of language.[2] Buttrick speaks of moves as a "series of rhetorical units." And also says, "All moves have an opening 'Statement' and some sort of 'Closure.' In between, moves have some kind of developmental pattern.[3] Though the term "point" is used in this study guide, (for reasons given below), preachers should be knowledgeable of the term "move."

Pericope—A passage of scripture, usually more than one verse, from which a text is obtained. A pericope may be as long as a chapter or even two or more chapters from a book of the bible. A text is rarely more than eight verses.

Point—A section of focus of a sermon; it is a specific element or idea. Modernly, some homileticians no longer use the term point when discussing sermon design. However, it remains the word most commonly used by novice and experienced preachers to discuss the sectioning of areas of a sermon, and movements in a sermon. When the term is used in this study guide, it concerns "making moves in a movement of language." I use the terms point and move interchangeably, throughout the study guide.

Text—A verse or verses drawn from a larger pericope that are chosen as the focus for a sermon.

Now, to encountering the whole person. By encountering the whole person, one is touching their emotive consciousness, not just their cognitive/intellectual consciousness. How does encountering the whole person differ from what is traditionally done when clergy preach?

Western culture's preaching tradition goes all the way back to classic antiquity and the oratorical methods of pre-Christian Greco-Roman culture. The rhetoric and oratory of classic Rome were designed to change people's minds, after which it was assumed that their behavior would change. It was abstract, as opposed to full of concrete images. The classic orators spoke to the logical thought processes, for the most part.

Encountering the whole person requires that we speak through experience to feeling (emotion) and intuition (hunches beyond human explanation), as well as to logical thought. With this type of encounter, we are doing more than *thinking* about God and the Word. It helps hearers *experience* the Word and meet the Lord for themselves.

This experiential approach requires as much biblical and theological study as does the traditional cognitive emphasis. The difference is that, once the academic type of study is done, the preacher is just getting started. The greater task of helping this learning to become an experience (not just a fact or an idea) still lies ahead. It takes great study for the preacher to see and hear and feel the Word, and it takes great labor and artistry to help others to do the same seeing, feeling, and hearing of the Word.

Abstract knowledge will not save souls, and folks can't be argued into faith. If intellectual genius saved folks, some great Christians we know would be in serious trouble. Knowledge is *sight*, and faith is blind (but not senseless) belief. Faith is a gift given to the formally educated and uneducated alike who seek it from God. To put it simply, we must love our Lord with all our "heart and soul and strength and mind"—with everything we've got—which is to say, holistically.

Analytical thought, however, comes *after* belief. Hebrews 11:6 says that those who seek a divine encounter must already believe that God is. Honest seekers who start out with minds full of atheistic or agnostic arguments will need respect and help. It will take a well-equipped preacher, or other consecrated thinker, to help such sincere seekers deal with their intellectual obstacles to faith. Then people can become open to the gift of faith, which may then come through an experience of the Word—and this only in the Creator's appointed time.

Those who preach depending on the persuasiveness of their logic may believe that they have succeeded, when they have, in fact, won only intellectual agreement from their hearers. Those who preach holistically will be used of the Holy Spirit to move hearers to holistic trust in God.

Have you ever said something like this about a sermon? "It was just as if I was the character in the story and Jesus was speaking to me personally." Or, "How did that preacher know what I was going through? I didn't tell anyone." This is experiential encounter, and it has been happening ever since our fathers and mothers began declaring the Word. Let us not forget that many of these preachers could not read or write.

And, if they were African American, for more than a century it was illegal in many states for them to attempt to do so.

Below are steps to aid this kind of picture painting with words and the kind of storytelling that pulls hearers into an experience of the story. Also, in preparing each sermon, use the "Vehicle for Holistic Encounter," which appears at the end of the chapter.

Begin a full exegetical study of your chosen text by first reading the bible passage as if you were watching it happen. On the third reading, look for all the details (colors, size, length, shape, etc.) that reach the senses and thus aid the hearer to visualize the scene.

A. COLOR
Genesis 37:3 becomes alive when you point out that Joseph's coat of *many* colors was as red as the apple you would have given your favorite teacher; and orange like the juice you drink for breakfast; green like the grass of a well-fed lawn; plus the coat had patches of sapphire blue, sunflower yellow, notebook-paper white, and shiny gold. Often colors are not given in scripture. This allows many opportunities for the preacher to provide them. The colors of things listed in the bible can typically be easily located through books or a Web search, and then there is always your imagination!

B. SIZE/LENGTH
Genesis 6:15 tells us that the dimensions of Noah's ark were at least 135 meters long (300 cubits); 22.5 meters wide (50 cubits); and 13.5 meters high (30 cubits). That's about 450 feet long, 75 feet wide, and 45 feet high! It could have been larger, because in the days of Noah, several larger-sized cubit measures were also used. A cubit was the length of a man's arm from fingertip to elbow. But, the 45-centimeter (18-inch) cubit is long enough to show the size of the ark. The deck area was equivalent to the area of about 20 standard modern basketball courts.

C. SHAPE
Have you ever preached the story of the woman who came to Jesus with the alabaster jar of expensive oil? How much more interesting would the story be, if you described the jar's shape and gave a general description of it? One preacher wrote about it this way:

> Alabaster was very expensive, like Chanel #5 parfum (not perfume). Parfum is the purest form and 15 ounces of Chanel #5 cost $1,850. The alabaster bottle resembled the figure of a woman. Perhaps the Goddess Bast (hence alaBASTer). In order for the precious oil to be released, the vessel (the alabaster jar) *had* to be broken. There was no cap that screwed on, or a top that sprayed a fine mist; nor was there a stopper that could be removed, so the jar could be preserved in pristine condition. That was the way the maker of the jar designed it.

> This is the way we are designed. We are vessels made by the hand of Almighty God for the specific purpose of the indwelling of the Holy Spirit. It is through trials and tribulations that we are broken. And, what is inside (the Holy Spirit), the precious oil, begins to pour out. Trials and tribulations don't come to just followers of Christ. They come to everyone. This is why we see people who have beauty, fame, and money that just seem to lose it, when trials and tribulations come. Their vessels have no precious oil inside.[4]

D. SMELLS

In the Parable of the Prodigal Son (Luke 15), the plight of the son is made more graphic when people both see and smell the food or "slop" that pigs are fed. The odor may be described as similar to that of uncooked chicken left on a kitchen counter in a 100-degree house, for a week. For the son to eat something that smelled that bad, he had to be desperate and starving. You could also state the color of the food he ate and describe its texture.

E. DISTANCE

A mile in the bible is 1049–1258 yards. That means that it would take the average person about 18 minutes to walk a mile. This distance information is helpful when preachers speak of characters traveling from city to city on foot and traveling to Jewish Festivals. When Jesus and the disciples walked from one city to another, a great deal of time was required if the cities were not close together. Jesus' insistence on going through Samaria, despite the hostile relations between Samaritans and Jews, introduces the factor of distance. To go *through* Samaria saved Jesus and the disciples a considerable hike (John 4:4). To cross over the Jordan, in order to bypass Samaria, was at least 40 miles out of the way.

F. TEXTURES

When one preaches about the crucifixion (on the old rugged cross), the texture of the ruggedness needs to be seen and felt. The two pieces of the cross were hewn by axes, not sawed or made smooth by modern machinery, such as a Black and Decker sander. Jesus' flesh was torn and ripped by huge wrought iron nails. It was also cut and scratched by splinters and the sharp-edged, unfinished wood.

G. SOUNDS

Exodus 8:1-32 discusses the plague of frogs that was sent against Egypt for Pharaoh's refusal to "let God's people go." The frogs filled the Nile, homes, and basically covered all of Egypt. Imagine hearing the croaking sounds of frogs day and night, and seeing and hearing them everywhere you went. They were in your front yard, back yard, on your roof, inside the house, and on every piece of ground on which you stepped. If the sheer number of frogs didn't drive you crazy, surely the croaking chorus of thousands of frogs would.

H. TASTES

The Song of Solomon 4:11(a) says: *"Your lips drop sweetness as the honeycomb, my bride; milk and honey are under your tongue."* Clearly, Solomon is attempting to describe a kiss he greatly enjoyed. By describing its taste as honey, the clear intent is to indicate that it was wonderful. Everyone knows that honey from a honeycomb is sweet. Maybe Solomon compared the kiss to the honeycomb because it was also sticky, in a good way. He couldn't easily wipe it off, and he didn't want to wipe it off. Have you ever kissed someone you loved like that, or had someone kiss you like that?

I. MOVEMENT

Throughout scripture, animals and people display movement. However, one might find this difficult to surmise from hearing many sermons. But this is simple to rectify. Consider that: flies swarm and jump from object to object and even on to people; David gets into a shooting stance and cocks a slingshot and it pops as the rocks fly; Martha scurries around the house and Mary chills (relaxes); Joseph wrestles with an angel (ahh, owhh) enough to dislocate his hip; frogs jumped around during the plagues sent against Egypt; and the list goes on and on.

Make sure that your sermon reflects the movement in your text. It may be pronounced, or you may have to use your imagination and ask: When the character did this, what movement occurred? Can I make his or her movement easier to see simply by saying what it was, or should I compare it to a movement with which my listeners are familiar to make it clear? Ask yourself, is this a movement that I can physically do in the pulpit? This is preaching without words, and it can be quite effective. Do not be afraid of using your entire body to preach. Our discomfort with using our bodies in preaching is due to certain dominant, western intellectual and religious traditions. **To remove such straitjackets from your body, ask yourself, How can my body get in on the good news?**

J. OTHER SENSORY DATA

There may be other sensory data, such as **temperature and humidity**, in the pericope, which can be important or useful. Pull them out.

Emotions: Read the passage again. This time, look for the deeper **feelings** of the various people involved (loneliness, jealousy, greed, fear, joy, depression, sorrow, pain, love). What was Jesus feeling when he wept over Jerusalem (Luke 19:41); when he said, *"Father forgive them, they know not what they do"* (Luke 23:34); or when he ran the money-changers out of the temple and turned over tables (Matthew 21:12-17; Mark 11:15-19; Luke 19:45-48; and John 2:13-16)?

Step 1 of creating holistic encounter: Try to place yourself in the biblical scene, and write down the feelings you would have had on the space provided on the worksheet. Then write down the feelings someone in your congregation or community would have had, **especially if the passage does not concern someone of your gender, age group, or class.**

Step 2: Decide what behavioral change(s) this bible passage is seeking to achieve. Is it perseverance (the ability to hold on); deeper faith; forgiveness; generosity? Make sure you know the answer. Remember, one of the main reasons a sermon loses its focus is because the preacher does not know what he or she wants listeners to DO after they have heard the sermon.

Step 3: Decide how many of the details above are necessary in the telling of the story, to achieve the behavioral aim in a sermon lasting 20 to 30 minutes. Underline the details that are required. Circle those which are optional. Do not feel badly about the details not used. Save them in a file, to be used at another time. No exegetical detail or insight is ever lost or wasted, unless it is not written down or is not remembered.

Step 4: Using a recorder, practice telling the story or painting the picture. You need not record your entire sermon. Use the details you believe are relevant to reaching listeners emotionally and cognitively, given the behavioral aim of your sermon. Listen to the recording and determine if it is an effective eye-witness account. Decide how to improve it, and then write down the word-picture, as you want to use it in your sermon. Try to avoid both overkill (using too many details) and understatement (insufficient detail) to make it come alive.

Also, regarding details, **please be aware that using more scriptures does not typically mean one is providing more details,** just more scriptures! Too often, when preachers are not sure that they have sufficiently made a sermon come alive (or proven some point they desired to make) and received the audience response they desired, they resort to rattling off one scripture after another. This will not help hearers, who will not be able to process the new content or the meaning of multiple scriptures tied to one or two points/moves in a sermon. Select a main text, bring it to life with appropriate details and succinct sentences, and stop there!

Doing all of this work may seem picky and time-consuming. You may believe that there is a shortcut that leads to a holistic, experiential encounter. There is not. You may believe that preachers do not prepare sermons in this way. But, the significance of these details is not in the details themselves. They are important in that they assist the hearer in entering into—"visualizing"—the story or other genre. Without details, the sermon waxes abstract or, worse, is blurry or vague. With details, the Word comes alive, comes "clear," and invites the hearer into holistic encounter.

Note: Use of tools such as the Libronix Digital Library (formerly Logos), other Web-based resources, and the *Bible Study Source-Book* by Donald E. Demaray, will provide colors for objects, sizes, shapes, textures, distances, etc. There are also many other books on the market that you can use.

NOTES

1. Frank A. Thomas, *They Like to Never Quit Praisin' God: The Role of Celebration in Preaching* (Cleveland: United Church Press, 1997), 31.

2. David Buttrick, *Homiletic Moves and Structures* (Philadelphia: Fortress, 1987), 23.

3. Ibid., 27.

4. "What's in Your Alabaster Box?" November 27, 2007. Online Blog—The Alabaster Box. Online location: http://thealabasterbox.wordpress.com/2007/11/27/the-alabaster-jar/ (accessed January 9, 2012).

A VEHICLE FOR HOLISTIC ENCOUNTER

1. Write down all the COLORS in your pericope. Be sure to find those colors that are <u>not stated</u> in the text. All objects (shoes, dirt, sand, plants, and even a person's skin) have a color.

Object or Person	Color

2. Write down all SIZES in the pericope, including sizes that are not stated in the pericope but could have been.

Object or Person	Size

3. Write down all SHAPES indicated in the pericope, including those not mentioned (as they rarely are).

Object or Person	Shape

4. Write down all SMELLS in the pericope, including smells that are not mentioned (few will be). Use your imagination and other sources to determine odors.

Object or Person	Smell

5. Write down all TEXTURES in the pericope, including textures which are not mentioned.

Object	Texture

6. Write down all SOUNDS in the pericope, including sounds not mentioned.

Object/Animal/Person/Nature	Sound

7. Write down all TASTES in the pericope, including tastes that are not mentioned directly (as when reference is made to food items).

Food/Beverage/Other Item	Taste

8. Write down other Sensory Data (Temperatures, distances, movement, etc.).

9. Write down all references to FEELINGS (emotions) in the pericope, and the people to whom these feelings are ascribed.

The Person	The Feeling (emotion)

10. Once you have completed a first draft, or a complete outline, **underline** all details needed (essential) and **circle** all details not needed (non-essential) for this sermon.

3

ARTFUL ORATORY: MAKING A SERMON COME ALIVE

A boring sermon is an iniquitous insult to an infinitely imaginative God
—Brad R. Braxton

Preaching is not simply the dissemination of information. Preaching is artful oratory that creates the conditions for an authentic decision about God. When people make the right decision about God, the consequence is shalom—God's intended wholeness for the creation.[1]

So, how does one create artful oratory, meaning how does one make a sermon come alive? Is it some special gift owned by very few? The answers are yes and no. There are great preachers who do have unique gifts for making the Word come alive. But, it is also true that there is a well-defined route that can be followed by most preachers that will yield good results. This disciplined approach is briefly presented here.

1. When Scripture comes alive, it is encountered as if it were just that—alive. For this to happen, one needs the ingredients of a real-life experience: colors, sizes, shapes, smells, textures, sounds, tastes, distances, temperatures, etc. These were discussed in Chapter 2. The great preacher who is described as one who can paint great word pictures is using these very data to help the hearer feel as if she or he is there in the biblical story or event. The story comes alive for the listener.

2. Producing vivid preaching requires discipline and being an avid reader. It is caught while reading the bible over and over and not just for preaching purposes. One also "catches" competency in word pictures while reading great literature such as Toni Morrison's *Beloved*, J.D. Sallinger's *The Catcher in the Rye*, Chinua Achebe's *Things Fall Apart*, Richard Wright's *Native Son*, Miguel de Cervantes Saavedra's *Don Quixote*, or Zora Neale Hurston's *Their Eyes Were Watching God*. Vivid pictures and the right phrases to describe them become etched in the mental repertoire of the reader, to emerge later, often unexpectedly. They become part of the natural tongue of the preacher. There are jewels of the word canvas that can even be found in cartoon strips such as *Dilbert*, *The Far Side*, and *Calvin and Hobbes* and certainly in books of poetry such as *Go Off and Split* by Nikki Finney, winner of the 2011 National Book Award for Poetry, or Poet Laureate Rita Dove's 1986 Pulitzer Prize-winning book of poetry, *Thomas and Beulah*.

The common characteristic of all these forms of writing is the desire of the authors to get and keep the reader's interest with vivid images. One thing is sure—the mind that is not regularly exposed to good reading material will be limited to the images and language of what little has been read, placing a tragic limitation on what a preacher is able to offer at the preaching moment. Wide contact with spoken and written words will deepen the reservoirs of a preacher's gifts.

Another vehicle that can be extremely useful for preaching is song lyrics, particularly the lyrics found in blues, country, sacred, and rap music. Too often preachers save song lyrics for the end of sermons or only use the lyrics of sacred music. However, good music comes in so many styles. In each case, the music catches one's attention because of vivid images. When preaching a sermon that focused on saving black boys, I used a verse of the song "Lord Knows" by the late Tupac Shakur to describe the hopelessness felt by too many black boys. (See the sermon in Chapter 10.)

3. The gift of verbal picture-painting is "caught" while reading in a particular way: experiencing the Word as an eyewitness. Instead of combing the Word or a book for ideas to preach, one simply turns on the sound and the "picture screen" from the pages. This, then, becomes the reader's own story, in Technicolor. When preachers say, "I can see Jesus in my mind's eye hanging there on the cross, limp between two thieves," listeners should see a real cross with real color, shape, size, and weight and a real body, made limp by the brutality of crucifixion.

4. In addition to word pictures, one needs to study how they relate to the broader central theme of a given piece of great literature. In other words, word pictures are not just to be seen; they are used to convey great meanings. But, great meanings are impossible for the preacher to convey unless the preacher knows what the great theme was for which a word picture was used in the first place.

The first place to start in reading for great themes is simply to read a lot of good casual reading books, such as J.K. Rawlings's *Harry Potter* series or Sieg Larson's *The Girl with the Dragon Tattoo* and *The Girl Who Kicked the Hornet's Nest*. One can then move on to more complex books and even to great literature. Little by little, one becomes more and more capable of seeing the message of a book. There is only a limited number of great biblical themes or folk doctrines (forgiveness, love, justice, grace, providence, redemptive suffering, etc.) being communicated, regardless of the number of good books one reads.

The ways in which themes are expressed will vary greatly, but one must keep in mind that *every* author is promulgating *some* idea or theme. Love is love, whether seen in Zora Neal Hurston's *Their Eyes Were Watching God* or Victor Hugo's *The Hunchback of Notre Dame*. Providence is providence, whether seen in Margaret Walker's *Jubilee* or J.R.R. Tolkien's *The Lord of the Rings*. Justice is justice, whether seen in Harper Lee's *To Kill a Mockingbird* or Shakespeare's *The Merchant of Venice*. Hope is hope, whether expressed in Nella Larsen's *Quicksand* or Frank McCourt's *Angela's Ashes*.

One cannot skim the bible, or any literature, only looking for good images, metaphors, or sermon ideas, any more than one can skim the bible overlooking contexts and hunting clever texts. But, preachers can make sermons come alive for others when the sermon has come alive for the preacher. Thus, it helps if preachers preach about issues that are important to them and that concern their context. However, it is next to impossible for one to speak knowledgeably and convincingly, even about those subjects which excite him or her, if he or she is not well-read. Additionally, the more selective reading the preacher does, and the more the reading preacher moves personally into the experiences on the pages, the more the preacher develops her or his own ways of using words to bring messages to life in eyewitness style.

It may take more rigorous scholarship to give eyewitness accounts than scholarly lectures. But, whereas lectures are seldom recalled, except by means of written notes, the preacher's word pictures become the hearer's own vision and experience. And, many people have been known to carry vivid messages with them all the days of their lives. This is the goal of all good preaching.

Many people today read less, but they see a great deal of good art and literature in movies. Whether you know it or not, many in your congregation are more likely to rent a film through a Red Box, buy one through their cable subscriber, buy one on DVD, or go to a movie theater than they are to read their bible in any given month. So, the preacher should not overlook motion pictures as a resource. Two books that can help are Craig Larson and Andrew Zhan's *Movie-Based Illustrations for Preaching and Teaching (101 Clips to Show or Tell)* 2003 and 2004 editions.

5. A good way to start learning how to identify BIG themes is to look at the big issues raised. It is then a relatively easy step to see what important questions are raised for the Christian faith. For instance, Spike Lee's film *Do the Right Thing* (1989) raises the Big theme of justice and the issue of racism. The movie is open-ended, providing the preacher with a launch for a sermon on Christian love; as opposed to racism, or on justice, as opposed to injustice. Think of the possibilities from this movie on doing the right thing as a backdrop for a sermon after a police shooting of an unarmed, non-combative citizen, or after persons are killed during a gang war.

Imitation of Life (1934, 1946, 1959), directed by John M. Stahl, is one of the most important films on Race and was named as such by *Time* Magazine in 2007. It also addresses the theme of family. The daughter (who has a very light complexion) of the black maid in the film decides to pass for white, which grieves her mother. Given the issue of family discord, and self-esteem issues with which so many teenagers wrestle, imagine using this film for a movie night for your youth ministry and then using it to preach on a Youth Sunday with Psalm 139:14 as a text: *"I praise you because I am fearfully and wonderfully made; your works are wonderful, I know that full well."*

If your church is not equipped to run video clips, likely you do have the resources to at least show graphics. The right graphics can work wonders in establishing the sermonic mood before, during, and at the conclusion of the sermon. They are particularly useful during high holy moments, for faith communities. One caution: too many different graphics during a worship service can be confusing. So, be clear about the aim of your message for the day, and then find one or two graphics that will definitely help embed your aim in the hearts and minds of the congregation.

Whether you use video clips, movie clips, graphics, or other aids in bringing your sermon alive, be sure to ground the sermon in the bible, not in a book, movie, or video. Although people enjoy good books, movies, and videos, they do not go to church to hear them as the primary source used for a sermon. Second, make sure your material is age and context appropriate. The images that will appeal to your youth or to your young adults may not appeal to your senior citizens, and vice versa, so some set-up by way of explanation may be required.

Portability and Fitting Sermons

This chapter concludes with a discussion of portability and fitting sermons, both of which were briefly mentioned in the introduction. Again, portability concerns the ability of a sermon to gain a hearing in any venue where the Word of God is proclaimed. To say a sermon is "fitting" means it is the right word, in the right form/style for a particular group of people, at a particular time in history.

Young preachers especially, and even older preachers often want to know, in so many words: how can I craft sermons that can be preached in small rural churches and at Westminster Abbey? Yes, one of these venues is at the extreme end of the preaching spectrum, since so few will preach there for so many reasons, but I am sure you get the point.

Much-desired portability is possible for those whose sermons:

• concern the Big themes/issues of the Christian faith community as they have come to us from the bible, the Church, and culture;

• are crafted with exegetical precision, designed with flair, and delivered with homiletical passion; and

• are always crafted with the understanding that a sermon may be heard in multiple venues by sister churches of all sizes, churches filled with people of various ethnic backgrounds, churches of various social classes, and those with varying cultural-historical backgrounds. Although a sermon may have to be altered stylistically to make it lend itself towards a particular venue, a style change is small, as compared to theological and related content changes and changes made to give a sermon focus, which are major changes.

For some African American preachers and even some preachers of other ethnicities, the issue is whether the sermons will be portable, if, for example, I am used to preaching to audiences that are verbally responsive and lively, and I go to venues that are quiet and reserved. The reverse is an issue of some white, Latino/a, and Asian American Christian preachers. There is a bottom line here: a preacher who preaches with passion and prepares substantive, well-crafted sermons about Big issues can preach anywhere and get a faithful/good hearing. Also, use of common sense helps. If a church is very quiet and reserved, you can turn the energy and perhaps your volume down a little. If a church is loud and energetic, turn up your energy.

I shall never forget being a seminarian and attending a four-day revival being preached by one of my then-seminary professors at Ebenezer Baptist Church in Atlanta, the church of Dr. Martin Luther King Jr. and Reverend Martin Luther King Sr. At the time, Dr. Joseph Roberts was the pastor. The revival preacher for the week was Dr. Fred Craddock, who, as most preachers know, is a white preacher and was in his sixties, when I heard him preach this message. On the first night, though it was more than 20 years ago, I can still remember that he preached "Did You Ever Hear John Preach?" I can still hear him describing John's garments, his repeated use of the word "riveting," and his description of snow falling in one of the illustrations he used.

I have also had the privileged experience of hearing African American clergy Reverend Charles Adams, a current and long-time pastor in Detroit and an instructor at Harvard Divinity School; the late Reverend Dr. Prathia Hall; and Reverend Dr. John Kinney, a current pastor and Dean of the Samuel DeWitt Proctor School of Theology at Virginia Union University, preach in university settings, small churches, conferences attended by thousands, and other venues. In each instance, all three easily gained a hearing.

All of these preachers have in common that their messages are portable and fitting. In addition to the three factors discussed above, each preacher also has a keen understanding of genres and an extensive vocabulary filled with colors, insight, intellect, eloquence, humor, and a well-developed understanding of the prophetic for their generation.

NOTE

1. Brad R. Braxton, "Interpretation for Proclamation: Working with the Book," unpublished lecture delivered at the 2010 Hampton University Ministers' Conference, Hampton, Virginia.

4

GENRES: WHY PREACHERS NEED TO UNDERSTAND THEM

Understanding genres is important to preaching and to creating effective sermons. As time-consuming as it may be, preachers must give serious thought to which genre they are using so that they will not select a genre that is inappropriate for the behavioral claim they want to make upon hearers and for the occasion. When one does not select a genre, nonetheless a genre *has* been selected. In other words, failure to make a decision is a decision to preach a mainly cognitive message, or to stumble around in confusion.

Jesus was the master of teaching by parables. The word parable covers a number of different ways of helping people to understand by means of concrete parallels. Jesus took abstract, even complicated ideas and made them plain by laying them alongside something that people could see with their eyes and/or something with which people were familiar. But, each parable had a special way of presenting the parallel. So, too, must we who preach have a variety of types of parallels.

All of the various types of parallels could be called genres, a word denoting a form of writing or literature. A poem is a genre, but, of course, one is not likely to preach a sermon using only poetry. A drama is a form of literature or a genre, but we seldom use it as a genre for preaching. On the other hand, a story or narrative is a very common genre. When we want to know if a person can preach, we even ask, "Can this person tell the story?"

Jesus discussed the hiddenness of the Kingdom and its future consummation. If he had tried to do it in the abstract, the explanation could have been complicated and subject to failure. Instead, Jesus used a story about an over-eager worker who wanted to "weed" the tares out from the young wheat. The Master calmly reminded his listeners that they could hardly tell the difference at this stage, so it would be best to do the separation at harvest, when the crop is unmistakable. Jesus started the story with the statement, "The kingdom of heaven is like . . .;" this parable type or genre is called a **simile**.

Narratives, like the Parable of the Prodigal Son, do wonders in explaining what is meant by abstract terms, such as "grace and forgiveness," and secular terms, such as "a second chance," "sibling rivalry," "living the BLING life," and "family issues." One can tell the same story with the aim of helping young adults come to themselves (appreciate having caring parents), or to help rigid fathers be more forgiving, or to help siblings get along. Stories were used in early cultures for specific teachings or chosen behavioral ends. These genres work well for the same purposes today.

When one knows how powerful the impact of a well-chosen genre can be, it is not hard to understand why it is important that a preacher knows which genre(s) he or she is using in a sermon, and for what purpose. The power of all genres lies in a combination of simplified, parallel meaning and personal identification with or entry into the action and meaning of the genre. So, if the Parable of the Prodigal Son is told with the purpose of moving persons to accept the Grace of God, hearers with problems like those of the Prodigal will both understand grace *and* accept it emotionally. The power of all genres lies in the way each offers hearers an opportunity to enter into an experience parallel to their own, and with the result that they come out of the experience blessed.

Every text one preaches should have such an opportunity for identification into or "coming on board" with the sermon by hearers. So, every sermon needs either one genre or more to attract people into an experiential encounter. The genre puts the message into a picture or image that hearers embrace and with which they identify.

Some texts have their own built-in genre. Hebrews 12:1-2 is an example. It is built on the genre called **metaphor**, and the writer of Hebrews chose a metaphor for what we now call "track and field." The writer leads us to see the saints in the stands and the runners on the track, each laying aside weights and preparing to run the distance. When we have suited up in our own minds, the writer moves us to run the Christian race with patience and to look to Jesus, who is the author of our faith, for the outcome of our race.

Some texts offer multiple genres. Select only one. Paul says, "*...I see another law in my members, warring against the law of my mind and bringing me into captivity to the law of sin which is in my members*" (Romans 7:23). There are at least two metaphors here (war and prisoner) which can supply the entire structure of a sermon. Paul calls himself a "prisoner" (and means it in a good way) in several texts (Ephesians 3:1, Ephesians 4:1, and Philemon 1:1). Using the "prisoner" metaphor could be tricky to use in a positive way, as Paul often intended, since there is so much negative cultural baggage attached to the word. If you choose the prisoner metaphor, you could discuss in a sermon what it means to be a prisoner of God and a prisoner to sin at the same time. That will take a great deal of sermonic work; but, it could produce a powerful message to which many hearers can relate. Or, you could simply discuss what it means to be a prisoner to sin and the arrival of Christ in one's life as the alternative to this reality.

The points or moves for such a sermon are easy to see:

Text: Romans 7:15-25; 8:1-2

Move/Point 1 Focus Topic Sentence: The Law opened my eyes and showed me how bound I was.

Move/Point 2 Focus Topic Sentence: There are consequences of being a prisoner to sin.

Move/Point 3 Focus Topic Sentence: I am no longer condemned to serve a life sentence of imprisonment, because I am in Christ and walk after the Spirit.

Celebration or Conclusion Focus Topic Sentence: Thanks be to God, through Jesus Christ my Lord, I have deliverance.

To prepare sermons with texts that use metaphors, one studies the text and then studies the metaphor. The power of the sermon lies in the clear image of the metaphor, as it symbolizes parallel aspects of the sermon idea. When the hearer relates to the metaphor, the image and message are easy to remember, aiding the recall of most of the sermon.

To thoroughly discuss the moves above, for example, one needs some knowledge of what it means to be a prisoner and a prisoner to sin. Any listener, if only from what he or she has seen on television, has some familiarity with what it is to be a prisoner. So, it will likely be expected that the preacher will use some current references that apply to physically jailed prisoners, as well as those that specifically apply to Paul as a prisoner of sin, and to us.

The next and not-often-recognized genre is the **stream of consciousness** genre. As one reads the Fifty-first Psalm, all one sees is prayers, but the entire psalm is an outpouring of the psalmist's deepest feelings. It can be read as an outpouring of one's own feelings and stopped at verse 12. Verse 10 can be used as a text with verse 12 as the conclusion or the celebration. Or, reading the entire psalm, verse 17 can serve as a text and verse 15 as a conclusion. Done either way, the value of the flow of consciousness lies in the way it helps the psalmist and the contemporary reader to get things off their chests or to engage in a kind of spiritual catharsis.

Of course, there are texts that haven't a shred of suggestion as to a genre. One has, then, to find a way to preach the text using a genre chosen by the preacher. The idea is that no text will come alive without some way to help people see and experience it, and that requires a genre of some sort.

When Paul said in Romans 8:28 that God *"works in everything for good,"* he did not give hints in the verse or its context as to what genre might be used to make it come alive. But, one can go to another text to find a good genre that will bring alive the behavioral aim. Genesis 50 contains a narrative (genre), which makes this abstract verse's meaning clear and can make it colorful. Joseph (Genesis 50:20) declares in celebration that the Creator took what was meant for evil and twisted out of it a great blessing: *"You meant it for evil, but God meant it for good."* This story is one of many that can supply a genre for a text that has a genre that is difficult to determine. We can also find stories in history and those from the present that illustrate the doctrine of Providence (God working in all things for the good of believers who are called according to the purposes of God). So, whenever a text does not contain a genre, go to another text to find a genre that will aid the main text you have decided to preach.

However, be careful that you do **not** end up preaching two separate texts! This can be tricky—but does not have to be. The main thing to keep in mind is that the second text to which you turned to make your main text come alive is not your main text. It is only there to make your main text come alive and easier to understand. If you go to another text to find a genre to aid your main text, especially if the genre you select is a story, do not attempt to tell the entire story. Hit some of its high points and then relate these points back to your main text. In the case above, it is Romans 8:28.

It may be difficult to tell whether a passage in the bible is the story of one person—a **character sketch**; or, a group of people—a **group study**. A character sketch concerns one person. It consists of a series of brief episodes in which this person's life illustrates a particular character trait that you want others to emulate or avoid. This trait becomes the behavioral focus for the sermon. In a group study, the focus is on the actions and attitudes of a particular group. The aim is to move the congregation, as a group, to follow or not to follow the example of the people in the scriptural passage.

In Mark 16:1-8 (and all of the synoptic Gospels for that matter), there is the story of a group of unnamed women. Because of their devotion to Jesus, they went to the tomb early Easter morning. This gained them the honor of being the first to know of and announce the resurrection. This shows that God sees and rewards the devoted service of unnamed women, even if society does not. Since characters in a group sketch may exhibit more than one character trait that you want listeners to exhibit, be careful to select one, or no more than two character traits, for your focus in any given sermon. In the case of the unnamed women, the character traits could be courage and devotion.

The story of Joseph in Genesis 50 contains a dialogue with his older brothers. Because it is also a narrative, it illustrates the fact that pericopies may contain multiple genres. This should not confuse the preacher. **The main genre is the one that includes the others** (i.e., in this case you have a dialogue inside a narrative/story).

In the case where passages contain multiple genres, always determine which genres are present and write them down. When the main genre has been determined, this becomes the major framework for the sermon at hand. The other genres fit inside this main genre. Do not make your sermon complicated. Stay with one genre per sermon until you become skilled enough to capably apply two. It typically takes five or more years of consistent preaching (at least twice each month) to become competent in the use of all genres.

As you prepare your first draft, or an extensive outline, remember that the main genre is the anchor. It is closely aligned with the text out of which it has come. Once the first draft or outline is complete, read the sermon to ensure that your focus did not wander from the main genre to a secondary genre.

A VEHICLE FOR IDENTIFYING GENRES IN SCRIPTURE

The following definitions and exercises are given to help you identify genres in scriptural passages.

Genre Type: **Metaphor**

A metaphor is a figure of speech founded on resemblance, by which an idea is transferred from an object to which it properly belongs to another in such a manner that a comparison is implied, though not formally expressed. Thus, "That man is a fox" is a metaphor. The reference in Hebrews 12:1 to life as a race is also a metaphor. (Note that Hebrews never uses the word "like," which often distinguishes a metaphor from a simile.)

Metaphor Exercise: Provide details that indicate you have selected a metaphor on which to preach.

_____

_____

_____

_____

_____

Genre type: **Narrative**

A narrative is a story that is told or recited. One knows that it is a story because it has a setting, a main character (protagonist), a plot of action (conflict), and a resolution of the conflict (end of suspense).

Narrative Exercise: Provide details that indicate you have selected a narrative on which to preach. (Look for a setting, a main character, a plot, and a resolution of the conflict.)

_____

_____

_____

_____

_____

Genre Type: **Simile**

A simile is the likening of two things which, however different in other respects, have some strong point or points of resemblance. A simile is also a poetic or imaginative comparison. Thus, "That man is *like* a fox" is a simile. Jesus often said, "The Kingdom of Heaven is like unto . . ." Whenever you see a "like" statement, you know that it is a simile.

Simile Exercise: Provide details that indicate you have selected a simile on which to preach.

_____

_____

_____

_____

_____

Genre Type: **Stream of Consciousness**

Stream of consciousness is the outpouring of one's innermost feelings. There is not a conscious attempt to establish a formal structure for what is said, yet structure is present. The Psalms include many examples of stream of consciousness writing and so does the book of Proverbs. Scriptural passages which contain streams of consciousness are typically spotted by the fact that there are numerous places where one can begin and end the passage, for purposes of selecting a text.

Stream of Consciousness Exercise: Provide details that indicate you have selected a stream of consciousness passage on which to preach.

_____

_____

_____

_____

_____

Genre Type: **Dialogue**

A dialogue is a conversation between two or more persons. The story of Jesus and the Samaritan woman at the well (John 4) includes a considerable amount of dialogue. Note, however, that it is part of a larger narrative.

Dialogue Exercise: Provide details that indicate you have selected a dialogue on which to preach. Name the persons speaking. (Dialogues frequently are found inside of other genres.)

_____

_____

_____

_____

_____

Genre Type: **Poetry**

A poem is a composition in which the verses consist of certain measures, whether in blank verse or in rhyme. It is also a composition in which the language is vividly imaginative. The New International and the Revised Standard versions of the bible present much of the books of Isaiah and Jeremiah in their original poetic form.

Poetry Exercise: Provide details that indicate that you have selected poetry through which to preach.

_____

_____

_____

_____

_____

_____

Genre Type: **Character Sketch**

A character sketch concerns one person. It consists of a series of brief episodes in which this person's life illustrates a particular character trait. This trait becomes the trait you want hearers to emulate or avoid.

Character Sketch Exercise: Provide details that indicate you have selected a character sketch on which to preach.

_____

_____

_____

_____

_____

_____

Genre Type: **Group Study**

In a group study, the focus is on the actions and attitudes of a particular group. The aim is to move the congregation, as a group, to follow the example of the people in the scriptural passage. Since characters in a group sketch may exhibit more than one character trait that you want listeners to exhibit, be careful to select only one character trait, or no more than two, for your focus in each sermon.

Group Study Exercise: Provide details that indicate you have selected a group study on which to preach.

_____

_____

_____

_____

_____

Genre Type: **Multiple Genres in a Scriptural Passage**

Many passages contain more than one genre. The pre-crucifixion narrative in Matthew 21:33-45 includes the narrative parable of the cruel farm owner. In the dialogue that follows, Jesus uses the metaphor of the stone that the builder rejected. Accordingly, one could choose to preach emphasizing any of the other genres.

The genre selected for emphasis becomes the main genre and the other genres in the passage become subordinate, or their existence is mentioned only in passing, **if at all**. For example, one could say: "As we are focusing on today's text, we encounter the parable of the cruel farm owner, also called a vine dresser. We may focus on that parable in the future, but for today, let's focus on the builder who was rejected."

Multiple Genre Exercise: From looking at your text and the former definitions given for different genres, name your main genre. Provide the details that indicate you have selected this genre. Next, using the former definitions as your guide, indicate each of the secondary genres present, and provide the details that indicate the presence of these genres.

Main Genre:

_____

_____

_____

_____

_____

_____

_____

_____

_____

Secondary Genre(s):

_____

_____

_____

_____

_____

_____

_____

_____

_____

5

EXEGESIS: WHAT DOES THE TEXT SAY AND MEAN?

How do we preach from the Book, the Bible, so that the living voice of God leaps off the page, calling us, comforting us, challenging us, correcting us and finally converting us to live as heirs of God and joint heirs of Christ? Depending on how we work with the Book, the Book can become a mechanism for entombing God in the mausoleum of the past, or the Book can become a means for enabling God to move into the present with vigor and authority.
—Brad R. Braxton[1]

Great interpreters are not those who have found the one meaning of a text but those who inspire others to voice their own response to the same text.
—Renita Weems[2]

For a variety of reasons, many preachers have difficulty giving more than surface treatment to a text that they select from a larger pericope. So, this chapter will mainly focus on exegesis—how the preacher gets to what texts say and mean through critical and historical analysis. As an exegete, the preacher must work with precision and not just passion. While doing so, the preacher must allow the bible to be a means of "enabling God to move into the present with vigor and authority," while also "inspiring others to voice their own response to the same text." These are two of the main aims of homiletical exegesis.

SELECTING THE TEXT

It sounds easy enough: just do it. Well, not so fast. Is it a holiday that you will be threatened with ignoring if you do not address it? Easter, Christmas, and Mother's Day come to mind. Is there something happening in your community that you would be seen as irresponsible for not addressing (a child murdered, a senior widow has her house foreclosed upon due to unscrupulous bank practices, the killing of a member of the church, etc.)? Is there something happening nationally that would cause you to be accused of having your head buried in the sand if you did not address it? For example, I guarantee that there was not an African American pastor in America who did not feel compelled in 2008 to preach (in some fashion) about Barack Obama's candidacy for the office of President. Fewer, for a variety of reasons, likely felt compelled to preach about President Obama's announced acceptance of Gay marriage.

Then, what about those who have to preach from a lectionary most of the year? Their text(s) have already been provided for them. Sure, they will be forgiven for foregoing the lectionary texts, if an occasion absolutely requires it. However, most often they have to preach the lectionary texts they have been given. Well, although many segments of my faith community do not follow lectionaries, it is not the worst way to prepare to preach. It can stop you from only preaching your favorite texts, place you in conversation with others, and greatly increase the likelihood that you will preach the majority of the bible. And, through social media, you now can actually be in dialogue with others around the world as you prepare sermons on the same texts. If you preach from the Revised Common Lectionary or another lectionary that uses multiple texts, remember, at a minimum for purposes of exegesis:

1. You are preaching as a member of a **community** of faith that has agreed to preach particular texts on particular days;

2. Although you are preaching as a member of a community of faith, you also preach in a specific community of faith. The two are not mutually exclusive, but there will be occasions when the two diverge on approaches to texts. I have witnessed this increasingly during the most recent economic downturn, as I read the sermons of black, white, and Latino/a United Methodist clergy whose sermons were placed on the Web; and

3. Although the preacher's focus will always lean more toward one text, when he or she has to address three or four texts in one sermon, the aim is to have the preacher do a thorough exegesis of each text and ultimately determine what similar thread(s) run through each, which is why they were united and selected as texts for a given season and day on a lectionary calendar.

. . .

Relative to African American, primarily Protestant clergy, let me be self-serving for a moment. In 2007, I gathered some of the best homileticians, cultural writers, historians, and worship leaders in the world to create The African American Lectionary, an online resource. It is designed to assist preachers in approaching the annual days of the Protestant, African American, liturgical calendar.

The African American Lectionary is a resource tool that not only highlights the African American ecclesial traditions and moments that creatively express the joy, freedom, and the challenges of being both African American and Christian (e.g., Watch Night, African Heritage Sunday, Usher's Day, and Women's Day), but also recognizes days on the liturgical calendar that are celebrated across a variety of ecclesial traditions (e.g., Advent, Christmas, Lent, Easter, and Pentecost).

By incorporating both the moments of significance across many African American ecclesial traditions and some of the traditional moments of any lectionary cycle, The African American Lectionary allows users to select from a vast array of material that will exactly fit their congregation's needs and expectations. So, if you are an African American preacher, or a preacher who needs to add African Americans to a conversation you want to have with a text, do consider using The African American Lectionary. This is a **free** resource that contained more than 11,000 pages of material as of summer 2012. It is only located online. The Web address is www.TheAfricanAmericanLectionary.org.

. . .

Now, back to selecting texts. How should preachers really select texts? There are many approaches that are perfectly fine. Some texts find you. They are laid on your heart or go racing through your mind and you're not sure why, but you can't stop thinking about them. Some texts you will find through prayer, meditation, living, and doing ministry. Some texts others find for you through their interactions with you. All are divine interventions!

When Selecting a Text, What Is Not Acceptable

It is not acceptable to select a text for preaching just because it is popular (e.g., the story of Joseph that I referenced above). It is not acceptable to select a text that one cannot theologically ground. Yes, one may preach from a creed, use a ritual (baptism or communion, for example), or even a song; however, they must be theologically grounded.

It is not acceptable to select a text just so that you are viewed as swag, clever, cool, hip, etc. Here, often the culture, as depicted in newspaper stories, on the Web, in popular songs, popular books, movies, etc., is driving the selection. I understand the desire for relevancy; surely no preacher should offer a sermon that is not relevant to his or her context. At the same time, relevancy is sometimes over-estimated or misunderstood. The Church, our communities, and our country would likely be a lot stronger if preachers concentrated on sermons that were counter-cultural ("turn the world upside down" and then right side up) and not just relevant. However, we must at least be relevant.

It is not acceptable to preach a text that you know absolutely nothing about and will not seriously study before preaching it!

It is not acceptable to preach a text that you primarily selected to bash those who disagree with your point of view, particularly if they are parishioners or people whose social classes, sexual orientations, or ethnic backgrounds, etc. are different than yours. Even when one aims to be prophetic, counter-cultural, etc., the Word of the Lord, the Good News, is still at its root about offering people a road map to the many manifestations of the salvation, love, and justice of the Savior who saved you. This does not have anything to do with being soft on sin. It has everything to do with understanding the ultimate aims of God and the Word of God.

Steps after Selecting a Text and a Brief Word about Hermeneutics

You have properly selected a text. It is occasion-appropriate. It is appropriate for your context. It is relevant and counter-cultural. You did not select it to bash anyone, and you are willing to study it well, if it is unfamiliar to you.

Now, read it aloud in several bible versions. Read it and listen to it. If you really listen, it will begin to speak, even at this early stage in the sermon development process. Once you have answered all of your questions and critically looked at the text historically and at its literary character, then read it again. You will hear things that you did not hear earlier, because at this point you will be more familiar with the text.

I would be remiss if I did not include in this chapter on exegesis a brief word about hermeneutics. Without being overly technical, hermeneutics is the art of interpretation, which includes understanding the meaning, use, and construction of words and understanding people.[3] Thus, again, the need for preachers to be well-read and to read across disciplines (not just theology and homiletics), as they preach and do exegesis. One should be aware that, as you are reading texts, your hermeneutical lens, whether you know it or not, is operative. By the phrase hermeneutical lens, I mean how one primarily views the world and that he or she uses this view as their interpretive framework in approaching texts. As Martin Heidegger (1889–1971) said, we bring with us a "fore-structure of consciousness" as we approach texts. This is our horizon. Just as we bring this to each text, so did each writer of a text, and it is their horizons that we exegete.

For instance, some preachers use as their lens relationships, others justice, some community, some power, some shared power, and the list goes on and on. In much of his preaching, Dr. Martin Luther King

Jr. used the "Beloved Community" as his hermeneutic or interpretive framework. Some use hybrids such as love and justice or ecology and peace. Whatever one's interpretive framework, the key is awareness of its presence and that it shifts as we age, encounter new contexts and experiences, and explore a variety of intellectual disciplines. For instance, if one tends to use *relationships* as their interpretive lens, they may need to augment (hybrid) their lens if they preach in chronically poor communities filled with children. They may need the interpretive lens of justice or shared power, too. Relationships, justice, and shared power are not mutually exclusive. This will require not just an understanding of the horizons of the prophets who spoke of such concepts in the bible and our own horizons, but also an understanding of our interactions in the world with entities (especially global conglomerates or systems) that have differing views than those of the biblical prophets, and that create outcomes that impact in death-dealing ways those whom God loves.

Now, to the really hard work. For this leg of the journey, the work of homileticians Thomas Long and Ronald Allen and that of theologians Catherine and Justo Gonzalez will be referenced. This phase of exegesis begins with Thomas Long's exegesis model for preaching. This model is likely now the most common preaching exegesis model used, though certainly the order of the steps change in various models.

THE EXEGESIS FOR PREACHING MODEL OF THOMAS LONG

A Quick Overview of Sermon Exegesis by Thomas Long

I. Getting the Text in View
   a. Select the text
   b. Reconsider where the text begins and ends
   c. Establish a reliable translation

II. Getting Introduced to the Text
   d. Read the text for basic understanding
   e. Place the text in its larger context

III. Attending to the Text
   f. Listen attentively to the text

IV. Testing What Is Heard in the Text
   g. Explore the text historically
   h. Explore the literary character of the text
   i. Explore the text theologically
   j. Check the text in commentaries

V. Moving Toward the Sermon
   k. State the claim of the text upon the hearers (including the preacher)[4]

I will not discuss every aspect of Long's approach, as some sections have already been touched upon and other sections are, I hope, self-explanatory. In addition to Long's model being a common sermon exegesis model for preaching, I am drawn to his approach because it closely resembles the exegesis approach for preaching that I learned in seminary. And, it works.

The one important exception I would take to Long's model has to do with the aspect of his approach that concerns "stating the claim of the text upon the hearer and the preacher," just before one begins to write a sermon. A claim made upon preachers and listeners may or may not be a behavioral claim and it may or may not be rooted in mutuality and solidarity. I would say, when you are through asking your questions and doing your exegetical work, know what you want hearers and the preacher to DO after having heard the message—and be able to state your behavioral aim in one short sentence. Long's model also does not give significance to the need for us to bring our "preassociations into consciousness." Those of us who have preached for a while may or may not do this automatically. However, the issue is important enough to raise it here.

Homiletician Ronald Allen addresses bringing preassociations into consciousness:

a. What emotions does the subject [issue raised by the text] of the sermon stir? Do these emotions predispose you toward the subject in any way?

b. Can you recollect experiences, memories, awareness of what others have said about the subject?

c. Suppose a member of the congregation looks into your eyes and asks, "Pastor, what do you think about this topic right now?" What do you say? Are you willing to risk the possibility that the conversation could cause you to change?

d. Do you have an intuition about where this sermon might go? Eventually you need to reflect critically on such hunches, but begin by getting them on the screen. [In other words, just acknowledge them in your mind and or write them down.]

e. Which of your preassociations seem most loaded, most charged, most capable of influencing the sermon?[5]

Understand that you will come to texts with preassociations. Particularly, be careful when you prepare to preach a passage that has been made famous and/or popular by a preacher you know. And be mindful of things you learned about texts as a child. Such teachings die hard, even when they are dead wrong. Finally, ask yourself: What is it about my identity that draws me to certain features/details in a text, while causing me to ignore others? For example, why are you drawn to the details in a text that concern or lead to subjects such as fornication, homosexuality, or the sexual mores of women, but not to texts that concern or lead to discussions of subjects such as gluttony, the evils of war, the merits of teens, greed, or how churches can help those who are in prison?

Now, more about Long's method and his point to reconsider where the text begins and ends.

Before I attended seminary, I had drilled into my head, in one way or another by preachers, Sunday school, and bible teachers: "Always read what comes before a text, what comes after it, and know about the book in which the text is found!" In other words, texts are never to be read, preached, or studied in isolation if one wants to do proper exegesis.

Long discusses it this way:

The Bible does not come to us in little bits and pieces, in individual texts and isolated pericopes. It comes as a canon, a set of documents that are themselves letters, legal writings, historical narratives, and so on. . . . We should look, then, with a slightly suspicious eye at the way we or the commentaries or lectionaries have cut our text. Examine what comes before the text, and what comes after it, to see if the surgical incision has been made at a responsible place.[6]

Long then gives the example of the story of the widow who gave to the church all she had, two copper coins (Mark 12:41-44). He points out that verses 41-44 are often used to extol the virtues of the widow's stewardship and sacrifice. This is not an incorrect thing to do. However, he importantly also points out that in the same pericope (verses 38-40) is Jesus denouncing religious leaders who devour widows' homes.

Also, never take a text out of context and do not accept it when others—not even commentary writers or lectionaries—do it. If you decide for some reason to narrow the focus of a pericope (especially a long one), or a text, just be aware that you have done this. Know why, and what you left out. Also, again, one's preassociations are important. In the Mark passage above, why might one be drawn to preach about the widow's stewardship and, not about those who devour the homes of widows?

UNDERSTANDING THE TEXT

Now, a few remarks about another aspect of Long's method—bible translations. The reason to establish a good translation of the bible, says Long:

> [I]s that every translation of a Biblical text is already an interpretation of that text. The vocabulary and thought patterns of the biblical languages do not square up one-to-one with contemporary languages, so even the best translations involve hermeneutical decisions and approximations of meaning.[7]

If one is not fluent in Hebrew and Greek, this problem can still be almost completely solved, if preachers simply use an inter-linear translation that has the original and the English language side by side.

I typically read a text in four or five bible translations, starting with the New Revised Standard Version (NRSV) and, most often, concluding with the Tanakh (the Jewish Study Bible). Most homileticians also recommend at least reading texts in the NRSV and the Tanakh. Steer clear of really paraphrased bible versions until you are well into the exegesis process. On the point of establishing a good translation of the bible, Long also says: "Be clear to read the footnotes in your Bible."[8] I won't belabor this point. It just needs to be done.

Understanding the text is the most difficult aspect of exegesis for the average preacher. The problem is made difficult by a variety of factors. First, many Americans never gain good reading comprehension skills prior to attending college. All of us know how bad K–12 public education has been in much of the United States, for the past 40 or so years. In and after college, reading comprehension is never discussed; it's *unfortunately* assumed.

Many who read this will say, "Poor reading comprehension—that causes exegesis problems?" Yes, it does. If one cannot comprehend what a scriptural passage means at a basic level, especially long passages with multiple, nuanced themes, this adds difficulty in an area (biblical exegesis) that is already difficult. Poor reading comprehension goes hand in hand with the writing problems often seen in seminary, as discussed above.

Second, the problem of exegesis is made more difficult by the inability of preachers to simply pay attention to texts and to the world in which preachers live. Here, I am reminded of black preachers who were never allowed to attend school and gain a formal education. However, neither slavery nor Jim and Jane Crow laws could stop them from paying attention and using their imaginations to fully see texts and ask questions.

I heard the late pastor Shelvin Hall of Chicago say on numerous occasions when I was but a teenager: "How in the world can a Black preacher go out into his [or her] neighborhood week in and week out and be lost for something to preach? Just pay attention. Sermons and issues are all around you—hollering at you: 'preach about me. Preach about me'!"

When is the last time you paid attention to the hint of pepper in the soup you ate? When is the last time you paid attention to the little child who always grabs your leg at church? When is the last time you paid attention to an elder, long enough to notice that the gladness has gone out of her eyes? When is the last time you paid attention to the flowers near the altar, to see the yellow daisies, the burnt-red roses, and the lilies, as they drooped? When is the last time you paid attention?

So, even if one has limited reading comprehension ability, at least pay attention to the world around you. This will greatly aid in one's ability to preach sermons that connect with hearers. It will also give you new approaches to texts that you have heard and or preached again and again.

Here are some tips to improve reading comprehension of biblical texts. First, of course, look up in a good bible dictionary any terms with which you are unfamiliar. Next, read the text aloud in several bible translations, and only one should be highly paraphrased. Then, recall instances in which you have heard the same text preached and or taught. Do **not** try to repeat points you have heard preached (even if you believe you can put your unique spin on them), or go to the Web to find sermons in which your text was used, until you have preached the sermon. Finally, remember as Long points out: "The punctuation of the text can be a good guide to syntactical meaning, but we should be warned that punctuation marks are later additions to the text and are therefore already interpretations of a sort."[9]

ASK QUESTIONS OF TEXTS

All homileticians tell students to ask questions of the texts. I would add that there are no stupid questions at this point in the process. Initially, this can be a lengthy process, but after a preacher becomes familiar with doing it, asking questions of texts moves much more quickly.

For preachers serving communities suffering oppression and those preachers who also want to sharpen their skills of hearing the voices of the oppressed and marginalized, please be attentive to the comments below of Justo and Catherine Gonzalez.

For a pericope, let's use Acts 5:1-16 (NRSV), which most know as the story of Ananias and Sapphira.

[1]But a man named Ananias, with the consent of his wife Sapphira, sold a piece of property; [2]with his wife's knowledge, he kept back some of the proceeds, and brought only a part and laid it at the apostles' feet. [3]"Ananias," Peter asked, "why has Satan filled your heart to lie to the Holy Spirit and to keep back part of the proceeds of the land? [4]While it remained unsold, did it not remain your own? And after it was sold, were not the proceeds at your disposal? How is it that you have contrived this deed in your heart? You did not lie to us but to God!" [5]Now when Ananias heard these words, he fell down and died. And great fear seized all who heard of it. [6]The young men came and wrapped up his body, then carried him out and buried him. [7]After an interval of about three hours his wife came in, not knowing what had happened. [8]Peter said to her, "Tell me whether you and your husband sold the land for such and such a price." And she said, "Yes, that was the price." [9]Then Peter said to her, "How is it that you have agreed together to put the Spirit of the Lord to the test? Look, the feet of those who have buried your husband are at the door, and they will carry you out." [10]Immediately she fell down at his feet and died. When the young men came in they found her dead, so they carried her out and buried her beside her husband. [11]And great fear seized the whole church and all who heard of these things.

¹²Now many signs and wonders were done among the people through the apostles. And they were all together in Solomon's Portico. ¹³None of the rest dared to join them, but the people held them in high esteem. ¹⁴Yet more than ever believers were added to the Lord, great numbers of both men and women, ¹⁵so that they even carried out the sick into the streets, and laid them on cots and mats, in order that Peter's shadow might fall on some of them as he came by. ¹⁶A great number of people would also gather from the towns around Jerusalem, bringing the sick and those tormented by unclean spirits, and they were all cured.

Now, here are my questions:

- Who wrote the book of Acts?
- What was the writer's intent in writing the book of Acts?
- Under what conditions did the writer and those to whom he or she wrote live?
- How did the community of the writer understand this pericope?
- Who was Ananias?
- Who was Sapphira?
- Who was Peter and what was his role in his community at the point of this pericope?
- Where does this scene take place?
- Were Ananias and Sapphira middle-class or wealthy by the standards of their day?
- Is it significant that Peter says that they lied to the Holy Spirit?
- How did Peter know they lied about the proceeds that they gained from the sale of their land?
- Although the husband and wife were talking to Peter, he said, "You have not lied to us [who is Peter referring to when he says, "us"?], but to God?"
- When Ananias dropped dead, they buried him the same day. How was that done?
- Peter tells Ananias he "lied to the Holy Spirit and to God." He asks Sapphira, "How is it that you have agreed together to put the Spirit of the Lord to the test?" What did he mean by that?
- How did Peter know that Sapphira would drop dead after lying as had her husband?
- Is it relevant that the text does not say that they wrapped Sapphira's body before they carried her out?
- What was Solomon's Portico?
- How or should I talk about people immediately dropping dead after lying to the Holy Spirit and God?
- What is the relevance of Acts 4:32-37 (**always read what comes before a pericope and what comes after it**). Acts 4:32-37 (NRSV) says:

³²Now the whole group of those who believed were of one heart and soul, and no one claimed private ownership of any possessions, but everything they owned was held in common. ³³With great power the apostles gave their testimony to the resurrection of the Lord Jesus, and great grace was upon them all. ³⁴There was not a needy person among them, for as many as owned lands or houses sold them and brought the proceeds of what was sold. ³⁵They laid it at the apostles' feet, and it was distributed to each as any had need. ³⁶There was a Levite, a native of Cyprus, Joseph, to whom the apostles gave the name Barnabas (which means "son of encouragement"). ³⁷He sold a field that belonged to him, then brought the money, and laid it at the apostles' feet.

- What should be made of verses 13 and 14: "*None of the rest dared to join them, but the people held them in high esteem. Yet more than ever believers were added to the Lord, great numbers of both men and women*"?
- Did Peter have healing powers, given that sick people were brought so that his *shadow* might fall on some, as he came by? Does this type of healing occur today through disciples of Christ?
- Is it possible to have Peter's discerning spirit in today's world?

That's an extensive list. Now, here are some additional questions that I would ask, because of my social location, ethnicity, gender, and the preassociations I bring to this text:

- Since Acts 4 concerns a community of believers who were striving for unity, and I will be preaching to an ethnic community of believers who need more unity, should I address this in my sermon? If so, why and how?
- How can I be sure not to oppress any group while preaching this text? Remember that oppressed groups are not struggling only against a particular person or group. They are "struggling against systems that prevent the fulfillment of God's purposes for all creation."[10] So, be sure to direct the sermon mainly towards oppressive systems, not mainly towards oppressive individuals. See Walter Wink's Powers Trilogy: *Naming the Powers* (1984), *Unmasking the Powers* (1986), and *Engaging the Powers* (1992) for help in this area.
- What is theologically liberating about this text and to whom? What is oppressive and to whom?
- How shall I relay this sermon to women, given their role in my church community, and their financial status in America?
- Does this sermon have anything to say to young people who are new to the faith and to the idea of giving large sums of money to the Church?
- Since this passage discusses money, what does it say to my community about money and to the larger society?
- Should this sermon speak about the obligations that churches and preachers have once they have received the tithes and offerings of the people?
- What will this pericope reveal if I do not read it in purely religious terms? In other words, what would the average reader, in and outside of my community (believers and non-believers), see in this pericope? Remember that the way the bible is read has made it a tool for divine grace and scripture-invoked violence. Also, remember that it is always good to keep others in mind as we do exegesis.

Justo and Catherine Gonzalez would likely also have us ask: Are there any great readings from the early Church mothers and fathers that are applicable to better understanding this text and the preacher's main issue of concern? Here's how they address this matter:

> [R]ecovery [meaning what was said by early Church mothers and fathers] is a difficult task, for from a very early date the process began by which those elements of the tradition that could not be assimilated into the status quo were suppressed or ignored. We have already referred to Eusebius's attempt to show that the persecutions were little more than a grave misunderstanding on the part of the Roman Empire. More recent historians have also read history in a similar manner. For instance, treatises on the ethics of the early church deal almost exclusively with sexual mores, lying, homicide, and so forth, but fail to take into account astonishing teachings of early Christian writers regarding property, the use and distribution of wealth, and the like. The reason for this is that the definition of what are "ethical" questions has been narrowed in our capitalist society, precisely so as not to include issues such as whether private property is morally correct, or what are the rights of the poor. On the basis of such a definition, historians of Christian ethics tend to ignore the very radical things that have been said in earlier centuries of Christian history, and thus give us the impression that today's radical questioning of the rights of property, for instance, is a new phenomenon, about which Christian tradition has little to say.

> The ideologically suspicious preacher is not quick to accept such a verdict, but rather asks a further question: Is the history of Christian ethics a faithful rendering of what ancients Christians actually

taught, or is it rather one more case in which the interests of the powerful are being served by what seems to be impartial scholarship?

. . . [A]lthough there is no doubt that a great deal of Christian tradition has been oppressive, it is also true that there has been a filtering of the tradition, a selective forgetfulness, so that what we now perceive is a distorted view of the past of the church.11

A final question: Relative to this text, where do I stand on the "oppressor-oppressed continuum"? The Gonzalezes point out:

We stand at more than one place in the oppressor-oppressed continuum. A Hispanic male may be part of the oppressed minority, but as a male he must also become aware of the oppression of women, both in his culture and in others. . . . In addition, women of every racial and national group need to encounter the views of other women—and there are now writings in translation that make that possible for English speaking readers. Therefore as each of us approaches the resources available from other groups, we must use our own hermeneutical circle to understand what these resources have to say.[12]

Now that you have asked the relevant questions of your pericope, please be aware that as you preach your sermon you will **not use all** of the considerations or answers to your questions. By answering the questions, you will now know your pericope well enough to come up with a strong behavioral aim. Second, after this exercise, you will know your text well enough to do a much stronger historical and literary analysis. Third, you will not just take the (never totally culturally neutral) conclusions of commentary writers at face value. Finally, because you have asked the right questions, after your historical and literary analysis you will know your pericope well enough to develop a sermon outline in which you are confident (even if you have to redo it a couple of times). **Always** do an outline, even if you plan to write a full manuscript. Do **not** just outline the passage in your head.

EXPLORE THE TEXT THEOLOGICALLY

Although she never attended college, my mother was the first theologian I met. The second was Mrs. Nadine Hooks, the teacher's aide for my eighth grade class. These women taught me how to reflect on my faith life and the teachings of the bible and the Church and my faith community. They taught me that the main focus of my life is always on God and on justice. Seminary aided in these tasks. Then, over time, I learned to persuasively preach theological issues.

Keep the Focus on God

The first task, if one wants to preach theological issues persuasively, is to keep the focus on God and God's relation to the world. Paul Scott Wilson says:

Too often as preachers we are tempted to think that we are preaching about a doctrine, or a truth, or a story, or a text, and we forget the more basic focus, that we are preaching God. Systematic theologians often agree that their appropriate focus is first on God, God's self-disclosure in the life, death, and resurrection of Jesus Christ, in particular, and in human history in general. In addition the focus is on human response to God actual and potential. . . . 1. Ensure that the issue, question, or subject is in fact theological (i.e. not psychological, sociological, historical empirical, etc.) and separate the theological element if necessary (i.e., anxiety is a theological issue when it concerns lack of meaning in life). 2. Clarify and interpret key terms . . ."[13]

While preachers will accept that the focus should be kept on God, they may not understand what this portends for the gospel preacher. They may forget that we only see God "through a glass darkly" and that God's ways are past our understanding. So, be careful. Ronald Allen explains this point in this fashion:

> Even texts that initially sound straightforward often turn out to be more complicated when we listen to them carefully. Psalm 136 declares that God's steadfast love endures forever. However, the same Psalm rejoices that God struck down the firstborn of the Egyptians, drowned Pharaoh's army in the seas, and killed several famous monarchs. These actions are strange expressions of steadfast love.[14]

This shows that when a particular pericope is used the preacher need always be aware of the area of God's character on which a sermon is focused.

Theological Methods for Preaching

While some preachers have learned that the focus is to be kept on God, that the subject matter for a sermon must be theological, and that they are to define and interpret key terms, many still struggle with theological method. Regardless of what you have heard, there is no one theological method and certainly not a singular one that can be used for preaching. So, what's a preacher to do?

Preachers preach in contexts (communities). It is up to the thoughtful preacher to remember that he or she is delivering theology for a particular reason, to a particular community, at a particular time in history. If your community is black and poor, perhaps your theology begins where systematic Liberation theologian James Cone would begin—with an understanding that God is the God of the oppressed. If you are a womanist preacher, perhaps your theology would begin where Deloris Williams would begin it—at the door of marginalized women of color, for they are the oppressed of the oppressed. If you are a feminist theologian, you might begin it elsewhere. Perhaps you would make the classical theologians your point of departure or the Revisionist theologians. Or, perhaps you would include facets of several of these theological schools of thought and add your own. This can become your theological method for preaching.

Whatever you choose as your theological method for preaching, be sure that God and God's relation to the world is the focus, be clear what aspect of the character of God is in the text; and, determine whether you need to add a text to reveal other aspects of the character of God. Be certain that the issue(s) you raise is (are) theologically grounded, and that those theologians who aid you in doing theology are relevant to the needs and concerns of your faith community.

Also, as part of your theological work, never forget that you are in dialogue (conversation) with others. You are in conversation with the congregation, perhaps a denomination, theologians, commentators, and so many others. They will arrive in the study with you and may meet you in the pulpit. They may totally agree with you on your stance on the issue that God will have you address on a given Sunday. However, they may not. What if the preconceived notions they have about an issue are wrong? What if you are wrong? Did the text and God lead you to a new understanding? Can you admit it? Can you preach it?

I've often wondered how white preachers (especially those in the south) who preached **against** slavery handled the tension that they must have felt from their churches, their community, their denominations, their institutions, and even their families. Well, God is still speaking and there are so many issues that remain unaddressed by preachers who choose not to live with the tension that such preaching will bring. Ultimately, although each preacher is in conversation with many others, his or her and your job is to acknowledge and respect all of the voices in the conversation, then determine what it is that God wants said at a given moment, to a given people, and say it!

Finally, as Ronald Allen points out, remember that culture is part of the conversation:

> Past and current events, movies, media images, hopes and tensions in the community, insights from politics, sociology, psychology – each is a genuine other who may contribute insights, questions, experiences, and images to the conversation. For example, a sociologist's research on spouse abuse should not singularly dictate a sermon, but it may help the preacher realize who needs to hear the news of God's love and how God's call for justice needs to be focused.[15]

BRIEF WORDS ABOUT HISTORICAL ANALYSIS AND LITERARY ANALYSIS

Historical Analysis

John Hayes and Carl Holladay are correct when they say there is "history in a text and the history of a text."[16] This means the preacher will need to know something about the period in which a book was written and the period in which the events in the book occurred.[17] Learn as much as possible about all of the historical levels of the text you select; noting, as Hayes and Holladay point out, that one text can have as many as four or five levels of history in it. The same applies to the book of the bible in which a text is located. Use commentaries and books dedicated to the Old Testament and the New Testament to aid in this work.

Next, historically speaking, ask what the biblical writer intended by writing this text. This question not only requires that a preacher know the history of a text, but also that he or she understand the import of this history, as the preacher declares his or her intentions through the text. When a preacher's intent for a text differs markedly in a sermon from that of the writer, the preacher must at least be aware that this is the case and know what this means for the development and delivery of his or her sermon.

Additionally, history fixes certain things in time. There are those who believe that the bible is to be taken as a literal document that does not change over time, but most who have made this claim were reading translations. The biblical landscape had been changed. What I believe typical literalists are really seeking to do (among other things) is to claim the "eternal truths" (also called perennial truths) of the bible—truths that can be applied for every age. Though admirable, even this aim is fraught with the difficulties of language and culture, which are always bound, in some way, by history. Also, language and culture always come with an accompanying worldview and interpretations based on that worldview.

Yes, we must be aware of the history of each text; but, that will not allow us to preach a sermon that is firmly fixed in the historical moment of the text, and it will not always allow us to tell if the text we are preaching presents a perennial truth or one that is contextually true. Battles over perennial truths will wage forever.

Listeners want to know some of the history of a text, but more than that, they want the preacher/exegete to present it for their generation. In *Homiletic Moves and Structures*, David Buttrick makes the point through the story of the Stilling of the Storm:

> If we explore the story of the Stilling of the Storm, we may bump into some odd first-century notions. Without doubt, the storm was understood as demonic. Water was after all a home for Leviathan, was primal chaos, and was given to sudden turbulence when stirred by demons who were

decidedly more than impish. If we accept the Bible's words as eternally valid, do we then announce in our sermon that sea-storms are produced by evil demons?[18]

We could make such an announcement and listeners, who have seen the Weather Channel, heard of global warming, and check the weather on their phones and tablets, would think we were kidding, a fanatic, or not a well-trained exegete. Time will not permit me to make an argument about whether Jesus walking on water should allow one to preach that anyone can walk on water; or whether women must always keep their heads covered in church, because they kept their heads covered at certain junctures of Church history; or whether the statement "Women should remain silent in the church" is a perennial truth. These are decisions that I will leave to each preacher. In the end, preachers, aided by the Holy Spirit, will determine what are eternal truths, depending upon their view of God, their view of humanity, their view of themselves, and their cultural and educational training.

Literary Analysis

Now, a brief word about literary analysis. I alluded to literary analysis of a text when I earlier spoke of the need to understand the language of a passage, its words, translations, idioms, and overall context. It should also be said that preachers should pay attention to the "nouns, verbs, commands, and descriptive phrases in every sentence. Unknown, unusual, or repeated words, phrases, and themes should be flagged for further investigation."[19] This work can be aided by using a bible dictionary or similar reference book. For instance, the *Eerdmann's Bible Dictionary* gives insight on many literary elements in a passage.

Remember, "A psalm is different from a proverb or a parable. Each of these types of literature has its own stylistic features and patterns of construction."[20] Refer to my discussion of genres in Chapter 4 for additional help with literary analysis.

USING COMMENTARIES

Now it is time for you to go to your commentary. You are ready. You have listened to the text. You have asked questions of the text. You have made notes of your observations. You have looked at historical readings concerning subjects that are your main interests in this particular text. You have listened for the voice of your congregation and your community. You know why this passage matters to you and your hearers at this time. You know about the passage historically and you understand it as a literary device. The more you read, the more you can feel the Holy Spirit urging you to get to it. Now, write the sermon, liberate some soul, offer some Good News, correct, and challenge. Get moving!

So, you go to your commentary to check what you have discovered, determined, and read. What is true? What is not true? What is unanswerable? Because you have done thorough work before racing off to read a commentary, a commentary can now provide you with answers you lack and likely more questions, without your having to fear that the commentator is driving the conversation and your sermon.

There are hundreds of commentaries that preachers can purchase (some on CD Rom) that will aid them as they prepare sermons. Here is a brief list:

- *The Interpreter's Bible Commentary Series* (2002) by Leander E. Keck is published by Abingdon Press and includes 12 volumes. You can also purchase the CD Rom and a very helpful index.
- *The Women's Bible Commentary with Apocrypha, Expanded Edition* (1998), edited by Carol A. Newsom and Sharon H. Ringe, is published by Westminster John Knox.

- *Interpretation: A Bible Commentary for Teaching and Preaching* (1995) is published by Westminster/John Knox. The entire set contains 43 volumes and sells for $2,500–$2,900, depending upon where you purchase it. The CD Rom containing all 43 volumes can be purchased for considerably less. Some individual *Interpretation* commentaries (hard copies) can also be purchased for about $25.00 each.
- *True to Our Native Land: An African American New Testament Commentary* (2007), edited by Brian K Blount, et. al, is a one-volume commentary of the New Testament. It is published by Fortress Press.
- A commentary you can use, if you are preaching from the Synoptic Gospels is the *Social Science Commentary on the Synoptic Gospels* (2002) by Bruce J. Malina and Richard L. Rohrbaugh.

For Contextual Analysis

- *Stony the Road We Trod: African American Biblical Interpretation*, edited by Cain Hope Felder. Minneapolis, MN: Fortress Press, 1991.
- *Everett Ferguson's Background of Early Christianity* (3rd edition). Grand Rapids, MI: Eerdmans Publishing Company, 1993.
- The Powers Trilogy: *Naming the Powers* (1984), *Unmasking the Powers* (1986), and *Engaging the Powers* (1992), by Walter Wink. Minneapolis, MN: Fortress Press.
- *Preaching Christ from the Old Testament: A Contemporary Hermeneutical Method*, by Sidney Greidanus. Grand Rapids, MI: Eerdmans, 1999.

For Exegetical Study

- *New Testament Exegesis: A Handbook for Students and Pastors, 3rd Edition*, by Gordon D. Fee. Louisville, KY: Westminster John Knox Press, 2002.
- *The Bible: Approaching the Text in Preparation for Preaching* (Elements of Preaching), by Mary Foskett. Minneapolis, MN: Fortress Press, 2009.
- *Biblical Exegesis: A Beginner's Handbook, 3rd Edition*, by John H. Hayes and Carl R. Holladay. Louisville, KY: Westminster John Knox Press, 2007.

NOTES

1. Brad R. Braxton, "Interpretation for Proclamation: Working with the Book," unpublished lecture delivered at the 2010 Hampton University Ministers' Conference, Hampton, Virginia.

2. Renita Weems, *Listening for God: A Minister's Journey through Silence and Doubt* (New York, NY: Simon and Schuster, 1999), 88.

3. For a basic primer on hermeneutics, see Richard R. Osmer, *Practical Theology: An Introduction* (Grand Rapids, MI: Eerdmans, 2008).

4. Thomas G. Long, *The Witness of Preaching*, 2nd edition (Louisville, KY: Westminster/John Knox, 2005), 70.

5. Ronald Allen, *Interpreting the Gospel: An Introduction to Preaching* (St. Louis, MO: Chalice Press, 1998), 122–123.

6. *The Witness of Preaching*, 73–74.

7. Ibid., 75.

8. Ibid., 77.

9. Ibid., 78.

10. Justo Gonzalez and Catherine G. Gonzalez, "The Neglected Interpreters," *In the Company of Preachers: Wisdom on Preaching Augustine to the Present*. Richard Lisher, ed. (Grand Rapids, MI: Eerdmans, 2002), 259.

11. Ibid., 253–254, 257.

12. Ibid., 259.

13. Paul Scott Wilson, *The Practice of Preaching* (Nashville, TN: Abingdon, 1995), 83. I did not address the need for the theological focus to be on humanity, for as Gerhard Ebeling put it in his commentary on the way Luther speaks of God, "What is said of God does not have to be applied later to man [people]. . . . What is said of God is addressed to man [people]." Gerhard Ebeling, *Luther: An Introduction to His Thought*. Translated by R.A. Wilson (Philadelphia, PA: Fortress Press, 1972), 248.

14. *Interpreting the Gospel*, 83.

15. Ibid., 73.

16. John H. Hayes and Carl R. Holladay, *Biblical Exegesis: A Beginner's Handbook* (Atlanta, GA: John Knox Press, 1982), 45.

17. Ibid., 73.

18. David Buttrick, *Homiletic Moves and Structures* (Minneapolis, MN: Fortress, 1987), 264.

19. *Biblical Exegesis*, 46.

20. "Interpretation for Proclamation: Working with the Book," 16.

Sermon Exegesis Process

1. Select a text. There are numerous acceptable approaches to selecting a text; most are fine to use. Make sure your text(s) is occasion-and context-appropriate. It is **not** acceptable to select a text that you do not know and will not study, mainly because it is popular, that you cannot ground theologically, or to bash those who disagree with your point of view.

If you use a lectionary:

- Remember that although you are preaching as a member of a larger community of faith, your sermon will be heard in a specific community of faith. Always respect both.
- If you are provided several text(s) on which to preach, find the common thread(s) that run through each text.
- If you are an African American preacher or want to be in conversation with African Americans as you prepare a particular sermon for a day on the lectionary calendar, consider using The African American Lectionary. It is a free online resource.

2. Determine where your text(s) begins and ends. Note where a translation or a commentary chooses to cut a text. You do not have to do as they did. However, know why you made cuts where you did. Read any verses that come before and after your text(s). Know about the book(s) of the bible in which your text(s) is located.

3. Establish a reliable translation. Read your text in several translations, especially the NRSV and the translation most used by your congregation.

4. Know your hermeneutical approach as you prepare to write a sermon. Indicate it below:

_____

_____

_____

_____

_____

_____

5. List the preassociations you bring to your text(s).

_____

_____

_____

_____

_____

_____

_____

6. State what about your identity drew you to this text.

_____

_____

_____

_____

7. Understand your text.

What details concerning your text do you need to look up in a bible dictionary?

_____

_____

_____

What important differences and similarities did translations show you about your text(s)?

_____

_____

_____

_____

_____

Review the punctuation of your text(s) in various translations. Write down significant differences, confusing punctuation, interesting punctuation, etc.

_____

_____

_____

_____

_____

8. Identify the questions you have about your text(s).

(a) Text one

_____

_____

_____

_____

_____

(b) Text two

_____

_____

_____

_____

_____

(c) Text three

_____

_____

_____

_____

_____

(d) Text four

_____

_____

_____

_____

_____

9. Identify additional questions you have of your text(s), given your gender, age, and social location (ethnicity, income level, physical location, and the faith community to which you belong).

_____

_____

_____

_____

_____

_____

_____

10. Identify what readings (if any) by the early Church mothers and fathers, can aid you in exegeting this/these text(s). If there is none, are there early readings by the Church mothers and fathers of your denomination or faith community that can aid you?

_____

_____

_____

_____

_____

_____

11. Explore your text(s) theologically. Keep the focus on God and God's relation to the world. What aspect of the character of God is shown in your text(s)? Is this aspect of the character of God in keeping with the behavioral focus you have selected for your text(s)? For example, if your focus is on mercy, a text that concerns the vengeance or even the justice of God may not work, without some explanation.

_____

_____

_____

_____

_____

_____

12. Identify which theological method (revisionist, liberationist, womanist, feminist, hybrid, etc.) you used to prepare this sermon. How do you know this is the method used?

_____

_____

_____

_____

13. Identify with whom (denomination, congregation, media, sociology, psychology, a significant event, etc.) you are in conversation, as you prepare this sermon. How will this impact the sermon you will prepare?

_____

_____

_____

_____

_____

14. Do your historical analysis.

- Be sure you know about the period in which your text was written and about the book in which it was written.
- Ask what the historical writer of the text intended, when writing the text.
- Does the intent of the writer(s) of the text(s) match your intent for use of the text(s)?
- Are you attempting to preach what you believe is a perennial truth? If so, how did you determine that it is?
- What will be the import on your sermon of preaching a perennial truth?
- Have you prepared your sermon for presentation for this generation? Are there things in your text that require explanation, because of this?

15. Do your literary analysis.

- Use resources to help you gain a firm understanding of the language in a passage and its translations and idioms.
- Pay attention to the nouns, verbs, and descriptive phrases in each sentence in your text.
- Flag unknown unusual or repeated words, phrases, or themes for further investigation.
- Use bible dictionaries and other reference books to aid you in this area of work.
- Revisit Chapter 4 that concerns genres and do the appropriate exercises.

16. Make use of good commentaries.

- Make sure that you do not go to your commentaries too early. Do the work that you need to do to become familiar with the text(s) first, without the aid of commentaries.
- Use a variety of commentaries to: answer questions you have; determine if there are questions that are unanswerable; determine what is true and not true; and, to see if there are important questions that you have not asked and major facts that you have missed (especially those that require that you alter your outline).

6

FOCUS. FOCUS. FOCUS.

The effectiveness of every sermon depends, among other things, on the ability of the hearer to follow the message and become involved with it holistically. This requires sermon focus by the preacher, but the failure to focus is one of the most common flaws of the American pulpit, along with the failure to present the Word in an interesting manner. Every element of the sermon has to fit together and flow smoothly. There cannot be detours and departures in one's flow of thought. The sermon as a whole and each of the parts of the sermon must be *focused*, and the behavioral aim has to drive the focus of the sermon.

After selecting the pericope from which one is to preach and selecting the text, one then selects a behavioral aim that is grounded in mutuality and solidarity. Always ask the question: What is it that the preacher and listeners are to "*do*" after they have heard this sermon? Exhibit deeper trust in God, pray more, be more honest, go and help persons in prison, etc.? Design your behavioral focus and sermon accordingly. Ground the sermon in mutuality and solidarity with your listeners.

Note that a behavioral focus is never stated in cognitive terms; by definition it must speak to the behavioral bottom line. Accordingly, a behavioral focus is never expressed in statements such as, "I want the people to **know** . . ." or "I want to **show** that . . ." or "I want people to **understand** that . . ." That is a solely cognitive focus, not a behavioral focus.

After a behavioral aim has been identified, everything in the sermon **must** be chosen for its contribution to the behavioral aim, which itself flowed out of the text. Anything which does not support the behavioral aim points to some other aim, with or without conscious intent on the part of the preacher. This is what is meant by a "detour" in the flow, no matter how clever, impressive, or humorous the detour may be.

If the sermon's main genre is a narrative, the next place to check for focus is the protagonist, or main character. When a sermon does not achieve its purpose, it may be because the protagonist has not been accurately identified. All too often the preacher does not give consideration to who is really the main character.

The main character must embody the behavioral aim. If you want the hearer who has strayed from home to return, the Prodigal Son is the protagonist. If you are preaching to help rigid, unforgiving fathers, the main character in the parable is the forgiving father. In either case, the story is told to give main focus to the character who does what you and your hearers are to do in your faith walk, as a result of the sermon.

Next, all of the material in each part of the sermon must be directly related to the **focus topic sentence** of that area of the sermon. This focus topic sentence will not typically be stated in a sermon as delivered, but it is placed in the outline and controls the contents of each point (move).

In the further development of the sermon outline, each move/point has its own focus topic sentence. The *focus topic* sentence does as the name indicates. It is designed to focus the writer on each paragraph within a section or topic in the sermon. And, the topic sentence provides the overall focus for the sub-paragraphs that will be written. If one's focus topic sentence is "Run the race of life with patience," the only topics (issues) that can be discussed under this entire section of the sermon are *running, the race of life,* and *patience.* In this case, it might be simplest to use the metaphor of distance running to guide the move since it is obviously present.

Each focus topic sentence, then, has its own sub-focus paragraphs ("a," "b," or "c"), vividly pouring out facets of that point. In other words, any information which does not *directly* speak to the focus topic sentence should **not** be placed in the sub-focus paragraphs. This exercise is similar to writing a well-focused term paper. When one gets what one is certain is a bright idea, and it conforms to neither a sub-focus nor a major focus category, it does not belong in the sermon, even if this is the best idea one has had all day, all week, or all month! At that point, the great idea is written down and placed in a sermon file to be used at a later date. Outline your sermon so that you can clearly tell where each point begins, where each sub-focus topic sentence belongs, and what the paragraphs under that sub-focus topic sentence should concern.

Anything which is not directly related to your focus topic sentence is a distraction, no matter how great the temptation to include it. All irrelevant words, illustrations, lists, poems, jokes, and stories should be deleted too. This should be done for **every** paragraph of your sermon. The rigor of checking each paragraph to make sure it speaks to the focus topic sentence for each move may seem arbitrary and time-consuming, but its practice pays off richly in impactful, uninterrupted flow. The power admired in preaching geniuses is often no more than the accumulated impact of their discipline in staying focused and interesting.

Although the following example is written in a three-point fashion, clearly, all sermons will **not** be crafted in a three-point fashion. There are so many ways to design an excellent sermon. I reference three-point sermonic design in this study guide because of its familiarity to all preachers. However, avoid deductive preaching when using a three-point sermon design.

Example:

Pericope: Hebrews 12:1-4
Text: Hebrews 12:1-2
Behavioral Aim: To move hearers toward persistence in the Christian life.

> **Move/Point 1 Focus Topic Sentence:** Lay aside unnecessary weights.
>
> Sub¶ a: Topic Sentence: Weigh everything that you carry.
>
> Sub¶ b: Topic Sentence: Many habits are too heavy for a Christian runner.
>
> Sub¶ c: Topic Sentence: Choose the lightest gear and discard the rest.
>
> *Notice that *laying aside unnecessary weights,* will be discussed in some way in each of the three paragraphs (a, b, and c).

Move/Point 2 Focus Topic Sentence: Run with patience.

Sub¶ a: Topic Sentence: The marathon of life is a long race.

Sub¶ b: Topic Sentence: Impatience and tension take energy from a runner.

Sub¶ c: Topic Sentence: A relaxed attitude of faith increases stamina.

*Notice that *running with patience,* will discussed in some way in each of the three paragraphs (a, b, and c).

Move/Point 3 Focus Topic Sentence: Look to Jesus.

Sub¶ a: Topic Sentence: Constantly looking back causes you to slow down and stumble.

Sub¶ b: Topic Sentence: Keep your eye on Jesus as the model runner.

Sub¶ c: Topic Sentence: People run best toward goals on which they focus.

*Notice that *looking to Jesus,* will be discussed in some way, in each of the three paragraphs (a, b, and c).

Celebration Focus Topic Sentence: The joy makes the strenuous run worthwhile.

Sub¶ a: Topic Sentence: Just to finish is a joy, because many do not.

Sub¶ b: Topic Sentence: The joy given by Jesus surpasses all other joy.

*Notice that *the joy that makes the strenuous race worthwhile,* will be discussed in some way in paragraphs (a) and (b) of the celebration.

PREACHING A SERIES

If preachers preach long enough, they will at some point decide to give variety to their preaching, by preaching a series. A series is three or more sermons that are connected by one overall theme and one overall behavioral focus. The individual sermons are assigned different titles and secondary behavioral foci. The series may have a single overall text, with secondary texts. It may have several texts connected by the overall theme.

The theme may be drawn from the bible, history, church doctrine, the sacraments, or a special occasion (a church's 100th anniversary, a church building campaign, etc.). Or, preachers may do a series on Easter, Lent, or Christmas, targeted toward a particular aspect of spiritual growth such as in the area of stewardship or the spiritual disciplines.

The point is that all series should be focused, which is why the topic of series preaching is placed in this chapter on focus. Focus greatly increases the impact of a series, its depth, and its reinforcement of the behavioral aim. The well-focused series moves hearers again and again through multifaceted goals, which are in fact only one unified goal.

An example follows. Notice that the overall behavioral aim remains threaded through each sermon in the series.

Series Pericope: Acts 4:32-37; 5:1-16; 2 Chronicles 7:13
Series Title: "Unite, Reverence, Repent, and Reap"
Series Behavioral Aim: To move hearers to reverence the giver of our financial gifts, by being generous and concerned for the welfare of one another.

First Sunday
Pericope: Acts 4:32-37; 5:1-16   **Text:** Acts 4:32-37
Title: "Of One Heart about Money"
Behavioral Aim: To move believers to unify and to take care of each other financially, by giving to the Church.

Second Sunday
Pericope: Acts 4:32-37; 5:1-16   **Text:** Acts 5:1-6
Title: "Reverencing the Giver of All Gifts"
Behavioral Aim: To move hearers towards acts that show that they reverence God more than they reverence gifts given by God.

Third Sunday
Pericope: Acts 4:32-37; 5:1-16   **Text:** Acts 5:7-11
Title: "Will We Repent?"
Behavioral Aim: To move hearers to repent for having improperly used financial resources.

Fourth Sunday
Pericope: Acts 4:32-37; 5:1-16; 2 Chronicles 7:13   **Texts:** Acts 5:12-16 and 2 Chronicles 7:13
Title: "When the Community Will Reap"
Behavioral Aim: To move hearers to accept that God will provide for those who turn to God and do so to aid their community.

A VEHICLE FOR GAINING SERMON FOCUS

Select the scriptural passage and text. After you have selected the passage and your text, practice writing one-sentence behavioral aims for the text. Remember that a behavioral aim is never stated in cognitive terms. Do not use words such as, "I want hearers to know . . ." or "I want to show . . ." or even "I want people to think differently about . . ." What do you want people to *do* after having heard the sermon? Does your text give you a clue?

Pericope/Scriptural Passage:

Text:

Practice writing a behavioral aim for your sermon:

(a) This passage is moving hearers to:

(b) This passage is moving hearers to:

(c) This passage is moving hearers to:

OUTLINE YOUR SERMON

Pericope: _____

Text: _____

Behavioral Aim: _____

Move/Point 1 Focus Topic Sentence: _____

_____

Sub¶ a: Topic Sentence: _____

_____

Sub¶ b: Topic Sentence: _____

_____

Sub¶ c: Topic Sentence: _____

_____

Move/Point 2 Focus Topic Sentence: _____

_____

Sub¶ a: Topic Sentence: _____

_____

Sub¶ b: Topic Sentence: _____

_____

Sub¶ c: Topic Sentence: _____

_____

Move/Point 3 Focus Topic Sentence: _____

_____

Sub¶ a: Topic Sentence: _____

_____

Sub¶ b: Topic Sentence: _____

_____

Sub¶ c: Topic Sentence: _____

_____

Celebration Topic Sentence: _____

_____

Sub¶ a: Topic Sentence: _____

_____

 Sub¶ b: Topic Sentence: _____

_____

Series Pericope: _____

_____

Series Title: _____

_____

Series Behavioral Aim: _____

_____

FIRST SUNDAY

Pericope: _____ **Text:** _____

Title: _____

Behavioral Aim: _____

Move/Point 1 Focus Topic Sentence: _____

_____

Sub¶ a: Topic Sentence: _____

_____

Sub¶ b: Topic Sentence: _____

_____

Sub¶ c: Topic Sentence: _____

_____

Move/Point 2 Focus Topic Sentence: _____

_____

Sub¶ a: Topic Sentence: _____

_____

Sub¶ b: Topic Sentence: _____

_____

Sub¶ c: Topic Sentence: _____

_____

Move/Point 3 Focus Topic Sentence: _____

_____

Sub¶ a: Topic Sentence: _____

_____

Sub¶ b: Topic Sentence: _____

_____

Sub¶ c: Topic Sentence: _____

_____

Celebration Topic Sentence: _____

_____

Sub¶ a: Topic Sentence: _____

_____

 Sub¶ b: Topic Sentence: _____

_____

SECOND SUNDAY

Pericope: _____ **Text:** _____

Title: _____

Behavioral Aim: _____

Move/Point 1 Focus Topic Sentence: _____

_____

Sub¶ a: Topic Sentence: _____

_____

Sub¶ b: Topic Sentence: _____

_____

Sub¶ c: Topic Sentence: _____

_____

Move/Point 2 Focus Topic Sentence: _____

_____

Sub¶ a: Topic Sentence: _____

_____

Sub¶ b: Topic Sentence: _____

_____

Sub¶ c: Topic Sentence: _____

_____

Move/Point 3 Focus Topic Sentence: _____

_____

Sub¶ a: Topic Sentence: _____

_____

Sub¶ b: Topic Sentence: _____

_____

Sub¶ c: Topic Sentence: _____

_____

Celebration Topic Sentence: _____

_____

Sub¶ a: Topic Sentence: _____

_____

Sub¶ b: Topic Sentence: _____

_____

THIRD SUNDAY

Pericope: _____ **Text:** _____

Title: _____

Behavioral Aim: _____

Move/Point 1 Focus Topic Sentence: _____

_____

Sub¶ a: Topic Sentence: _____

_____

Sub¶ b: Topic Sentence: _____

_____

Sub¶ c: Topic Sentence: _____

_____

Move/Point 2 Focus Topic Sentence: _____

_____

Sub¶ a: Topic Sentence: _____

_____

Sub¶ b: Topic Sentence: _____

_____

Sub¶ c: Topic Sentence: _____

_____

Move/Point 3 Focus Topic Sentence: _____

_____

Sub¶ a: Topic Sentence: _____

_____

Sub¶ b: Topic Sentence: _____

_____

Sub¶ c: Topic Sentence: _____

_____

Celebration Topic Sentence: _____

_____

Sub¶ a: Topic Sentence: _____

_____

Sub¶ b: Topic Sentence: _____

_____

Pericope: _____ **Text:** _____

Title: _____

Behavioral Aim: _____

Move/Point 1 Focus Topic Sentence: _____

_____

Sub¶ a: Topic Sentence: _____

_____

Sub¶ b: Topic Sentence: _____

_____

Sub¶ c: Topic Sentence: _____

_____

Move/Point 2 Focus Topic Sentence: _____

_____

Sub¶ a: Topic Sentence: _____

_____

Sub¶ b: Topic Sentence: _____

_____

Sub¶ c: Topic Sentence: _____

_____

Move/Point 3 Focus Topic Sentence: _____

_____

Sub¶ a: Topic Sentence: _____

_____

Sub¶ b: Topic Sentence: _____

_____

Sub¶ c: Topic Sentence: _____

_____

Celebration Topic Sentence: _____

_____

Sub¶ a: Topic Sentence: _____

_____

 Sub¶ b: Topic Sentence: _____

_____

7

THE ART OF DEVELOPING TITLES, INTRODUCTIONS, BALANCE, TIMING AND IMPACT, AND MORE

TITLES

Sermon titles need to be chosen carefully. Haphazardly chosen titles may mislead hearers, causing disappointment, disinterest, and/or confusion. Care in the choice of titles can draw better attendance, because titles can raise the interest of those who see them on the church marquis, in the order of worship, or online. Good titles also have the function of making a sermon memorable. Most importantly, titles can serve to orient listeners toward the direction the preacher wants to take with a text.

Several guidelines apply to the process of developing a sermon title:

1. Keep the title simple and brief. Long titles are distracting. More than five words are typically too many! When pulling a title from a text, keep in mind the length and make appropriate adjustments.

2. Give a title to the sermon *after* you've finished the first or second draft (as you name a baby after it is born). Don't spend a lot of time on titles before you write or outline the body of the sermon and the conclusion.

3. In determining a title, avoid cleverness for cleverness sake. Secular song titles are poor choices for sermon titles, unless they are seriously connected to texts and your behavioral aim. The secular-based title may be remembered, but will the sermon?

4. If at all possible, draw the title from the text. This will reinforce the memory of the text. When the text does not yield a title, lines from great hymns or other theologically grounded sacred music can be good sources (and these songs may also serve as the invitational hymn). From time to time, there are slogans or phrases from popular culture that can be effective as titles. Caution, this is rare. And, remember, these typically bring with them secular baggage.

5. Remember your behavioral focus when selecting your title.

6. Avoid negative titles! Negative titles can cause people to develop negative thoughts about the sermon and perhaps the preacher. Negative titles also make it difficult to reach a positive result. For instance, if your aim is to increase prayer by members, prepare a behavioral aim that is positively stated to achieve this aim. You would not phrase the behavioral aim as "to stop hearers from failing to pray." Instead it would be "to

move hearers to increased prayer." Your aim would be coupled with a positive title. Negative titles also tend to lead to negative sermons. Even sermons that challenge hearers need not be negatively focused.

Here are some examples of bad titles from scriptural texts, great hymns, and culture:

- "The Curious Journey of Jesus"
  Pericope: Luke 22
  Text: Luke 22:39-44
  Problem: It is difficult for people to remember and identify with opaque words such as curious, as it is used in this title. So, even before the message begins, the preacher has created a barrier, be it small or large. Also, such a title will require defining for a congregation. Avoid titles that require more than a sentence or two to explain them. It's best to develop titles that do not require any explanation.

- "Make Sure She Is a Help Meet"
  Pericope: Genesis 2:18-25
  Text: Genesis 2:18
  Problem: This one is tricky. At a quick glance, it may appear that this title is not problematic. However, it presents problems. Given that we live in a sexist world, why wouldn't a preacher give attention to a weightier issue such as the lessening of sexism? But, let's suppose that a pastor wanted to address to men the issue of selecting a good mate. This title would still not be a good one to select. Why? Failure to do a proper study of the words "help meet" will lead to improper defining and usage of the terms. I bring this up because I have heard this text preached on numerous occasions and have rarely heard the terms used with clear explanation of their original Hebrew meaning. Also, the term "meet," *kenegdo* in Hebrew, has multiple meanings that have to be reviewed carefully, along with the context of the text and other texts where the word is used. My guess is that after much study, only few male and female preachers would come up with a reading of Genesis 2:18 similar to one I saw in a feminist article that can be backed up by the Hebrew meanings of the words "help" and "meet": *It is not good that man should be alone. I will make him a companion of strength and power who has a saving power and is equal with him.*

- "The Consummation of the Kingdom"
  Pericope: Revelation 20
  Text: Revelation 20:4-6
  Problem: There are numerous problems with this title. First, it contains two words that are not commonly used in everyday conversation. The first, "consummation," is simple enough to define using its secular meaning. As a religious term, it is more difficult to define. The second word, "Kingdom," is difficult to define as a religious term. Second, there are so many views concerning the ending of the Kingdom of God that one can get confused attempting to coherently explain each of them, especially using a pericope that is apocalyptic and filled with symbols. Such texts must begin with bible study sessions. However, even after teaching such a text in bible study, it is still not recommended, due to the difficulties that arise with just the announcement of this title.

- "I Come to the Garden Alone"
  Pericope: Mark 14:32-42
  Text: Mark 14:32-36
  Problem: This text, according to the preacher who preached it, comes courtesy of a song that is beloved to many, "In the Garden." While the preacher is right about the song being beloved by many, it is also unfamiliar to many, as it was written in 1912. And, to my knowledge it has not been regularly sung in

American churches since the 1970s. Although the unfamiliarity of a song to a group is a hurdle that can be overcome, there are other problems with using this song as a title. The song concerns a person in a metaphorical garden in joyous personal meditation with Christ. The scripture, which also features an event in a garden, concerns Jesus in agonizing prayer that he be allowed to avoid death. Ultimately, he agrees to yield to the will of God, but his desire was to avoid the cup of death. Clearly, these two garden scenes are dramatically different and would take the thoughts of hearers in disparate directions as they attempt to integrate the two, using this text. Why select a title that is so problematic?

- "I'm a Fool for You"
  Pericope: Hosea 2–3
  Text: Hosea 3:1-4
  Problem: Here we have a title pulled from a song from pop culture. The song is titled "Fool for You" and is sung by Cee Lo Green, with Melanie Fiona. Using songs from culture is always risky, as they bring with them cultural baggage. In this case, this is not why the song does not work. The problem presented here by the song is exegetical. The Hosea passage, as most bible readers know, concerns God's undying love for Israel. God prods Hosea to forgive his wife, Gomer, who is repeatedly unfaithful to him. Such forgiveness by Hosea, which he sees as unthinkable, still does not begin to match God's level of forgiveness for Israel. Yes, the song concerns a man's undying love for a woman and this is shown in the text. However, using the term "fool" to describe Hosea's love of Gomer logically suggests that God's forgiveness of and love of Israel also is foolish.

Here are some examples of good titles from scriptural texts, great hymns, and culture:

- "Friends Take Friends to Jesus"
  Pericope Luke 5:16-26
  Text: Luke 5:17-26
  Why It Works: This pericope tells the story of a group of men who carry a man who has Palsy on a mat to Jesus for healing. Exegetical work will show that it took some work to get the man to Jesus. Hearers will easily agree that only friends would do what the men did to get the man with Palsy before Jesus. The text encourages hearers to also exert some effort to introduce their friends to Jesus. The title also works because most hearers will agree with its premise.

- "Jesus Paid It All"
  Pericope: 1 Peter 1:13-19
  Text: 1 Peter 1:18-19
  Why It Works: This title is taken from the well-known song, "Jesus Paid It All." It is found in most hymnals. This familiarity allows portions of the song to be used to introduce the sermon or it can be used in the celebration or the conclusion. The song is quite old, having been written in 1865, and even though it is a familiar song, many may not know more than the refrain of the song. However, no more than the refrain is really needed. This title also works because it allows preachers to teach a significant doctrine of the Church—the doctrine of Atonement about which many are confused and or unknowledgeable. 1 Peter 2:24 will also work as a text using this title. The pericope would be 1 Peter 2:18-25.

- "For Such a Time as This"
  Pericope: Esther 3:1-12 to 4:1-17
  Text: Esther 4:12-17

Why It Works: This title is found within the text at verse 14. Titles found within texts are easy for listeners to remember. This title also works because it allows preachers, in an open-ended fashion, to discuss current events with which their community is concerned.

- "The Charge Is Still the Same"
Pericope: 2 Timothy 4:1-8
Text: 2 Timothy 4:1-5
Why It Works: This title was used for a Pastoral Installation service. It worked in this instance, because of the well-known act called the "Charge," which is typically given to Protestant pastors as they begin their tenure at a new church. In several bible versions, the word "charge" is present in verse one. This text also works because it shows the historical continuity and scriptural basis for the office and work of a pastor. Pastors and churches are helped by seeing historical continuity in the life of the Church, and, by seeing scripture affirmed during a Pastoral Installation service.

- "The Worms Got Him, But. . ."
Pericope: Acts 12:1-24
Text: Acts 12:18-24
Why It Works: This is the story of Peter's imprisonment by Herod and his escape from jail with the aid of an angel. At verses 23-24 it says: "And immediately, because **he** had not given the glory to God, an angel of the Lord struck him down, and he was eaten by worms and died. **But** the word of God continued to advance and gain adherents." The "he" in verse 23 refers to Herod; his destruction is explained in verse 23 and in verse 24 what occurred to his body "he was eaten by worms" is indicated. The "but" refers to the word of God continuing to advance and gain adherents for the Church. Again, this title works because its words are found within the text, thus making it easy to remember. It also works because it is a clever way to explain that those who work against those who are seeking to do the will of God will not succeed.

- "You Are a Piece of Work"
Pericope: Psalm 139:1-24
Text: Psalm 139:13-14
Why It Works: Most have heard the slang phrase, "You are a piece of work." Typically, when used, it is intended to cast aspersions upon a person. Through this title and text, a negative phrase is turned into a positive one. Psalm 139, at verse 13, speaks of our being "fearfully and wonderfully made." This is the way God created us. This title is easy to remember because it is a well-known cultural phrase, and it works because it can help hearers gain a positive attitude about themselves, regardless of the negative ways others view them.

INTRODUCTIONS

Introductions should introduce sermons—no more, no less. To do this, there are a few rules that one should follow:

1. Remember, the introduction is to introduce the sermon. It is the set-up for what is to come. A very common error is the giving of a summarization of the sermon points (moves) in the introduction. There are few preachers who are skilled enough to do a summary of their sermon without telegraphing the resolution of the issues. Leave something for people to anticipate. Layer the sermon and build it, move by move. Here are some examples to be avoided:

- *"I stopped by this morning to tell you that whatever you're going through, Jesus is the answer. If you're sick, he's a doctor. If you're in trouble, he's a lawyer. If you're afraid, he'll give you courage. All you need to do is trust him and he'll always come through for you."*

The mind of the person in the pew says: "Thank you very much, Reverend. Now that I have the answer, I can go home." And, although they may not actually walk out the door, they may go home while still sitting in the pew. If you are able to bring them back on board the message, and then fail to persuasively articulate your behavioral aim by a thorough treatment of your text, you will have lost them twice.

- *"This morning I want to tell a story about a man who knew how to trust the Lord, no matter what happened. His name was Job."*

This information removes all of the drama from the sermon.

- *"This morning I want to remind you that the Word of God requires that every person repent and be baptized to gain salvation."*

The Word of God does not make these requirements for one to gain salvation.

Here are some examples of good introductions:

- *"Even though money is on everyone's mind these days, we still don't really like to talk about it, especially not in church. But, since so many of us are encountering problems dealing with money—getting it, saving it, knowing what to spend it on, teaching our kids about it—I believe it's time we had a frank discussion in the Church about money. Say Amen if you agree." (Text: Acts 5:1-12)*

- *"We continue to turn on the television, read in newspapers and magazines, and see on the Web, stories about preachers who are caught up in one scandal or another. From illegal drug use to sexual dalliances, to sexual abuse of children—what in the world is going on here?!! Why are those who are supposed to stand as spiritual pillars disappointing God and the Church so badly? Well, I believe our texts for today can explain why this is happening and offer solutions to the problem." (Texts: Romans 7:14-25 and 2 Timothy 4:1-15. For a pastors' conference.)*

2. Make the introduction to the sermon brief. If one is in a place where she or he is not known, it may be necessary to talk a while to gain rapport with the congregation. But, this is introducing the preacher, not the sermon. With the exception of story sermons (stories introduce themselves), one should get to the text as quickly as possible. In recent years, especially during revivals, I've heard more and more 50- and 60-minute sermons. These sermons are typically accompanied by long introductions. Even a long sermon does not require a long introduction. Also, too often listeners cannot tell where the introduction ends and the body of the sermon begins. This is a focus issue. The preacher and listeners should be able to clearly discern all movements (introduction, beginning, middle, and end) of a sermon. A focus problem is typically made worse by long introductions.

Although the introduction is brief, it is very important. It is an integral part of the sermon, as is the conclusion. The introduction serves the important purpose of claiming the congregation's attention and focusing minds on the issue that the preacher has selected for focus. All of this should be done, in most cases, in about five sentences. Notice that the sample introductions above have no more than five sentences. This is not a rigid rule. Introductions for sermons of 30 or 40 minutes may go as high as eight or nine sentences, but the quicker one gets to the text the better.

BALANCE

Balance (the quality of even flow requiring sermon points that are relatively equal in length) and timing (the quality of ascending interest and impact) are necessary elements of drawing and keeping hearers meaningfully involved in a sermonic experience. For those fortunate preachers who take outlines seriously, balance can be evaluated in a preliminary way at the outline stage. For those who use complete manuscripts, balance should be evaluated at the first-draft stage of the sermon and certainly checked again once the sermon is fully prepared.

At the outline stage, one can usually detect if his or her first point or first section is much longer or stronger than the other points in the sermon. If so, this is a balance problem that will ultimately create a timing problem. If the second point is stronger than the third, this too is a balance issue that will yield timing problems.

A longer sermon point is often caused by the fact that it is predominantly negative (negative material is much easier to produce than positive and thoughtful material). Typically, this also means that one is spending too much time stating a problem. This is easier to do than providing practical solutions, or than saying one does not have a solution. When one sermon point is longer than the others, excluding the conclusion, this can also be due to redundancy, brought about as one tries to explain a complex or difficult issue. The redundant preacher covers the same ground, using different words and even different illustrations to say the same thing.

Finally, balance problems also can occur because a preacher is discussing a subject about which he or she is very knowledgeable, and therefore has much about which to say, but crams too much of what she or he knows, into one section of the sermon. Similarly, when discussing an issue about which he or she knows very little, balance issues arise when the preacher rambles in an attempt to articulate and organize his or her thoughts.

In addition to the above means of detecting problems with balance, there is a simple test that can be performed. **If one is preaching a 20–25-minute sermon, it should be no longer than eight double-spaced pages.** Each page will contain 53 lines. The introduction receives a quarter of a page. Each of three moves (points) receives roughly two and a quarter pages, and the conclusion receives one page. This general pattern of proportioning would apply to sermons of any length and sermons with fewer or more points.

Another aspect of balance has to do with **meter** within a given move, or even just within a sentence. One sees meter problems when a list of names or adjectives, for example, includes two-syllable words and four-syllable words, or some other assortment of syllable counts. The human ear tends to want sameness in a series, so far as accents and rhythm are concerned. This means that a list or series should be metered in somewhat the same way one would meter the lines of a poem.

One can err by making **lists** too long. After the ear hears and the mind has to store more than five things on a list, it is hard to remember anything additional on the list. So, if lists are used and the preacher wants them remembered, the lists should be short and few per sermon.

If a list is given not because it is to be remembered, but to drive home a point, that is another matter. For instance, in describing God's love one might use a list of 10 descriptors. Hearers will almost instinctively know that the aim is not to have them remember the entire list, but to place in their consciousness the vastness of God's love. When lists are used in this fashion, length is expected. But, even in this case, be careful; do not include too many of this type of list in one sermon. And, if you include this type of list, make sure it is properly metered.

A final aspect of balance has to do with the **length of stories and illustrations**. In sermons where a story accompanies each point (move), care should be taken to keep each story to two (certainly no more than three) minutes. If this precaution is ignored, the longer story, if told well, will dominate and throw the entire sermon out of balance. Also, a well-crafted sermon does not need one story or illustration per point (move), to make it come alive; and a 25-minute sermon should not contain more than three stories or illustrations.

TIMING AND IMPACT

At the outline stage, it is also possible to identify timing problems. That is, even though the sermon has not been fully written, one may be able to sense that one move has higher impact than the proposed conclusion. The outline should then be rewritten to place the highest impact at the conclusion. Build in impact as your sermon proceeds.

Two questions often arise regarding impact. One is: "Suppose I don't use an outline, or suppose I begin by writing in a free-flowing stream-of-consciousness fashion and *then* write an outline?" In either case, one should evaluate impact at the earliest possible opportunity. Look at the points that have been used to make the sermon come alive; and, see to it that the one with the highest impact comes last and flows effortlessly into the conclusion or celebration. If the strongest song, story, illustration, or demonstration you have will not function as material for your conclusion or celebration, it should be placed in the sermon file for later use.

The second question is, "How will I know which move or point has the highest impact? I thought that was in the hands of the Holy Spirit." On the one hand, it is true that the Holy Spirit is the source of authentic impact. On the other hand, the pulpit is not the only place where the Holy Spirit visits. It is hoped that the preacher will sense the movement of the Spirit as he or she prepares the sermon. If a move (point) has strongly stirred the preacher's consciousness, all other things being appropriate, it will likely do the same with hearers. If in the study this stirring move was originally first, then it is time to write a new outline in which this move comes last, unless you have other points (moves) that are even more stirring.

Here is an example of a poorly timed outline:

> **Pericope:** Matthew 21:28-31
> **Text:** Matthew 31a
> **Behavioral Aim:** To move hearers to examine themselves by deeds done and instead of mainly by words spoken.
>
> **Move/Point 1 Focus Topic Sentence:** The first son said no, and then changed his mind.
>
> Sub¶ a: Topic Sentence: The first son flatly refused to work.
>
> Sub¶ b: Topic Sentence: The first son re-thought his answer.
>
> Sub¶ c: Topic Sentence: This son went and worked for his father.
>
> **Move/Point 2 Focus Topic Sentence:** The second son said yes and didn't work.
>
> Sub¶ a: Topic Sentence: The second son gladly agreed to work.

Sub¶ b: Topic Sentence: The second son got preoccupied.

Sub¶ c: Topic Sentence: The second son never showed up for work.

Move/Point 3 Focus Topic Sentence: Many *supposed* sinners will enter the Kingdom ahead of the *supposed* righteous.

Sub¶ a: Topic Sentence: Jesus asked which one did the will.

Sub¶ b: Topic Sentence: The priests and elders had no choice.

Sub¶ c: Topic Sentence: Jesus surprised them by indicating who will enter first.

Celebration Topic Sentence: Jesus decides who can reign with him.

Sub¶: Topic Sentence: Because it's all up to our merciful Savior, Jesus, every sinner saved by grace has a chance to reign with the King of Kings. I'm glad you have a chance. I'm glad I have a chance.

The above outline appears correct, since it follows the sequence of the parable exactly. The problem is that the disobedient son is discussed *after* the obedient son, which turns the flow of the story downward. Deal briefly with the father's problem and the first son in the first move. Then, deal with the second son in the second move. After this, deal with the first son again in the third move.

This flows perfectly into the third move about others who seemed to say no but did obey in their own way. So the revised outline reverses the order of Move 1 and Move 2 and turns the flow of the story upward.

The concerns of timing also include appropriate use of elements such as alliteration, humor, repetition, and rhyming. These elements, when overused, take from the message. Overuse may even drive away interest and attention, because some will hear the excessiveness as overkill.

Alliteration is the design of sequences of words, all of which begin with the same letter (consonant): "Discipleship is daily, disciplined, and delightful living for our declared deity." Alliteration should be used sparingly when it just happens to occur naturally and/or when it will add to the effectiveness of a sermon.

A trend of the past decade or so involves preachers going out of their way to alliterate the main, not the sub-moves, in a sermon. Sometimes this is done even if the alliteration is forced on to the selected pericope. Such forcing usually means that after these alliterated points are declared, they are not adequately addressed. Below are examples from actual sermons.

Alliteration of an outline using Genesis 37:1-36; 39:1-23:

Move/Point 1 Focus Topic Sentence: Joseph is tested by being tossed in a pit.

Move/Point 2 Focus Topic Sentence: Joseph is taunted by a temptress.

Move/Point 3 Focus Topic Sentence: Joseph triumphs from trials because he has favor.

Another example using 1 Samuel 16:13:

Move/Point 1 Focus Topic Sentence: The anointing is more important than the appointing.

Move/Point 2 Focus Topic Sentence: Another man's armor will not be appropriate.

Move/Point 3 Focus Topic Sentence: Appreciate every moment of your divine assignment.

Repetition of a text or lines of a text is fine, but too much repeating of a scripture, parts of a scripture, or a sermon idea is never acceptable. Also, be aware that listeners can often tell if a preacher is using repetition to fill the time due to inadequate preparation. However, repetition for effect can be very useful, especially just before concluding a sermon.

Humor comes in two forms: jokes and humor inherent in a pericope. Jokes are often used to warm up an audience. However, it is sometimes possible to use humor to strengthen a message, if the humor is properly focused on making an important point in the sermon. For example:

> A nine-year-old was doing a great job reciting the ten commandments in front of the adult Sunday School. Everyone was so impressed by her memory and how articulate she was. She reached the seventh commandment and said, "The seventh commandment is, "Thou shalt not *admit* adultery." The adults laughed under their breaths. Her teacher whispered, though not that softly: "Mary, it's "Thou shall not commit adultery." With a quick reply, Mary turned to her and said: ""That's not what my father said."" (Used in a sermon on rearing a child; Text: Proverbs 22:6).

There is much potential humor inherent in biblical scenes. And it not only draws a laugh, it renders the scene unforgettable. Do not overlook the humor inherent in a pericope. In fact, do a careful read of each pericope, so that you do not miss the humor. Dean Burkey's book *Holy Laughter! Humor in the Bible* can aide you in uncovering humor in pericopies.

Rhyming is rare in most sermons, but one branch of the African American pulpit tradition still does it sometimes, as they whoop. The material is spontaneously cut into metered lines and amounts to a kind of blank verse. Done in the main body of a sermon, it may be wasted and prone to signal the premature end of the sermon. Nevertheless, when rhyming is done among persons whose cultural expectations include whooping, it can be very effectively used as another wavelength for celebration.

Rhyming can also be effective when found in poems that are made part of a sermon, especially when the poems are well-written and on point. Much of the country remembered for days after (for various reasons) the words of Reverend Joseph Lowery, who gave the benediction at the inauguration of President Barack Obama: "Blacks will not be asked to get in back, when browns can stick around, when yellow will be mellow, when the red man can get ahead . . . and when whites will embrace what is right." These were lines very familiar to black preachers and their community. The reverse of what was meant by Lowery, and has often been said in rhyme by black preachers to show racist sentiments of others is: "If you're white, you're right. If you're yellow, you're mellow. If you're brown, stick around. But, if you're black, stay back."

A VEHICLE FOR DEVELOPING TITLES, INTRODUCTIONS, BALANCE, TIMING AND IMPACT, AND MORE

Titles

1. After you have finished preparing your sermon, look at the text. Pick out its main phrase or clause. Ask, Will it be familiar to a large number of those who will hear the sermon? Is it short enough for a title, or can it be shortened for a title? Count the number of words in your title. If there are more than five words, pull out the least important. Think of hymns or use the index of a good hymnal to find song titles for words that express the sentiments of your text and are familiar to your hearers.

2. Check your title. Is it clear? Will it help people remember the text and/or behavioral aim? Be brutally honest with yourself. Rewrite the title if necessary.

3. Does your title exegetically match your text?

4. Is your title inappropriate, meaning does it come with too much baggage? (It can be exegetical baggage or cultural baggage.) Is it too negative? Does it exclude certain groups of people?

5. Is your title vague, convoluted, or too difficult to be easily understood?

6. Is your title positive?

Write several possible titles for your sermon. Review the rules above and select the best of those you have written.

_____

_____

_____

_____

_____

_____

_____

_____

Introductions

1. Review the pericope and text. Make sure you have not summarized the sermon. Ask yourself, Have I **prepared** the people for what is to come (**without telling** them what is to come)?

2. Check to see if there is anything in the introduction that points in some other direction or raises some issue other than the main issue about which you will preach.

In five to eight **short** sentences, write your introduction.

_____

_____

_____

_____

_____

_____

_____

_____

_____

_____

Balance

1. After writing your first draft, look at the length of each point. Your points should be approximately equal in length, except the conclusion, which will be shorter. Delete material which throws the sermon out of balance. Always cut negativity first. If you cut good material, take care to mark the material carefully, indicating what your first intention was for it and why you could not use it for its originally intended purpose; and then place the excised material in a file.

2. Check the meter of the sermon, paying particular attention to any lists. Are there lists that you need to meter? Are there lists that you need to delete? Are there lists that need shortening? Indicate them below.

_____

_____

_____

_____

_____

_____

_____

_____

_____

3. Check the number of stories in your sermon. If you are preaching for 25 minutes and you have more than three stories, you have too many stories. Note that in a sermon of between 15 and 30 minutes, no story should take more than two minutes to tell, unless, of course, it is a one-story sermon. Good stories that are deleted should be placed in your sermon file. Once a story has been identified for deletion, so it can be found again, indicate the point of the story, and note *why it could not be used* for its original purpose. **Then, put it in your sermon file that is hopefully on CD or a server that is secure for saving and/or backing up material, or use the cloud storage system.**

List your stories that need to be shortened and/or those you need to delete.

_____

_____

_____

_____

_____

_____

Timing and Impact

1. Regardless of the order in which the events of a pericope are given in the bible, alter the order if the story flows downward. (See the text on page 88.)

2. After writing your first draft, review each section of the sermon to make sure your strongest songs, stories, examples, and/or illuminating details fall in order. In other words, build to your best story, illustration, or demonstration.

3. Check so that you are certain you do not have two or more sermon conclusions. If you decided to conclude with a song, select only one song with which to conclude.

4. Check so that you are certain all alliteration, jokes and humor, repetition, and rhymes used in your sermon actually aid listeners in better grasping the message and in becoming involved in a holistic, experiential encounter. Delete as necessary.

Indicate alliteration, jokes, humor, repetition, or rhymes to delete:

_____

_____

_____

_____

_____

_____

8

INCLUSIVE PREACHING: REACHING ALL

The topic of inclusiveness is always thorny, precisely because it forces societies to deal with their minorities and outcasts and calls for change. Inclusiveness challenges the exclusions decreed by the wielders of power. However, since the gospel is for the whole world and more importantly God is for the whole world, the preacher dare not offer sermons that exclude. Excluding people is not usually a matter of barring entry to a sanctuary or any sacred preaching space; or, not allowing people to partake of the sacrament. Rather, exclusion occurs most often when people who should be drawn by the Good News are repelled, because both overt and subtle signals drive them away. One of the most common means of driving people from preaching and the church is the use of *language* that excludes people and or belittles them.

Although some preachers have now seen the wisdom and justice of inclusive language, far too many continue to preach sermons which use language that is not inclusive as to gender, race, and sexual orientation. And, far too many still think others are being "picky" or overly sensitive about unimportant technicalities, if they raise the issue of inclusive language. Far too many preachers are prone to misjudge the role and power of words, and to let tradition, media, and other instruments of power overrule sensitivity to the "least of these." This could be termed yielding to the pull of the world and not the pull of the Word. The job of every preacher is to mature spiritually and culturally and to help congregations do the same. If you serve a congregation that is sexist, racist, or homophobic, your job is to help them mature and learn how to be inclusive.

Part of learning to be inclusive is recognizing that language is not set in stone. It changes constantly through the natural dynamic of usage. Thus, words mean different things at different points in history. Phrases like "mail carrier," "fire fighter," and "Mother God" may, in time, become quite acceptable even though one may have grown up using the terms "mailmen," "firemen," and "Father God." The words of the late Peter J. Gomes are helpful on this point:

> …What is remarkable is that the text itself remains fixed and unchanged. No new translations have emerged to clarify textual issues. No hidden or lost manuscripts have been unearthed that would unfix long-settled opinion. No startling revelations external to the biblical text have been discovered with radical new information. What has changed, however, is the climate of interpretation, indeed, the lenses with which we read the texts and the tales. The texts have not changed but we have, and the world with us. Scripture, like Jesus Christ himself, may be the same yesterday, today, and forever, but our capacity to read scripture and to appropriate Jesus Christ and his teachings is not. No one in contemporary America, except perhaps the most hard-bitten white supremacist, would read scripture with regard to race in the same way as Southern Baptists read it a century ago, or even

thirty years ago; and no one feels that some travesty of scriptural integrity has happened because of that fact. The racial theories based on the tortured inheritance of the sons of Noah, upon which racism in America and apartheid in South Africa were based, have yielded to Saint Paul's notion of the new creation in Christ and the transformed, renewed mind. The very same Paul who was seen as the apostle of the status quo is now also, and by the same people, seen as the apostle of liberation.

It is not scripture that has changed, but rather the moral imagination by which we see ourselves, and see and read scripture. It is that moral imagination that tells us what we see and hear in scripture, and it is that same imagination that allows us to translate those transforming images into the world in which we find ourselves. The moral imagination, liberated from slavery to the literal text, also liberates from the cultural captivity of context both ancient and contemporary, and is informed by nothing less than what Christians call the Holy Spirit. That is why the book of Hebrews describes scripture as "sharper than a two-edged sword." This is why scripture is described as "the lively oracles of God."[1]

Another factor in how language impacts us, and how we respond, is power. Such a terrible word as "Nigger" was quite acceptable in Southern and other newspapers, within easy memory of many alive today. But, African Americans gained the right to vote and became leaders in many capacities, and now no respectable newspaper would dare use such a word. The power of the courts, the ballot box, and purchasing power have moved that word out of acceptable and proper usage by most. This is also an indication that cultural mores are not fixed in stone either.

There are still some words in fairly common use which insult ethnic groups and people of good-will, just as "Nigger" once did African Americans. Words like "Jap" and "Spic" and "Chloe" may not be used in the media, but they are all-too common in the conversations of all classes of persons. The preacher must move against such usage. But these are the obvious cases.

Pronouns expressing gender may also be belittling. Because they are so often used in certain settings, they are hard for some to detect in every day speech. Women are ignored, for instance, in the choice of pronouns referring to God. We usually refer to God as "He" and use the phrase "mankind" to refer to humanity in total. Yet, Genesis 1:27 says that male and female were created in the Creator's image.

All of these show a lack of sensitivity, and insults diminish the respect that we should give to one another. Some of these biased and negative usages are so deeply embedded in our culture, and so commonly used within cultural groups that they are ignored, as being offensive. Or, they are thought to be acceptable, as the word "Nigger" once was. However, it is the responsibility of the preacher to pay attention, not ignore, and teach and preach to hearers to do more to embrace their brothers and sisters. These often quiet blows of negativity and exclusion through language increase the distance between hearers and the Word and the preacher. They undermine the holiness of the speaker and the self-esteem of some hearers, and they are just plain wrong. And, before moving forward, let me be clear, while men are most often found in roles of power in the Church, and therefore have more opportunities and are most often guilty of excluding, too many women are also guilty. They exclude through male-centered language and by engaging in practices and protocols that exclude women and others.

DEFINITIONS FOR OUR DISCUSSION

What is meant by "*gender inclusiveness*" in preaching? While gender inclusiveness certainly means not degrading anyone or any social group, ignoring them in sermons, or devaluing them through texts, it is much, much more than this. To be gender inclusive means, at a minimum, that one takes seriously the notion of all persons being created equal, totally equal, by and in the image of the Creator. It means that one takes seriously the notion of the beloved community, not a community where hierarchical structures place some at the top and others at the bottom. Further, it means that preachers should admit that they have been reared and educated in a world that has historically placed women and others in positions subordinate to white men; and preachers must then do their part to lessen such discrimination and subordination. Black male preachers, Asian male preachers, Indian male preachers, and Latino male preachers, all of whom have been subordinated to white male preachers, must also take responsibility for their subordination of women, especially women in their own ethnic community.

And, for those who preach in North America, it means declaring the Word in a society which for centuries devalued all women of color and in too many cases does so even today. This was not because the Creator willed it or ordered it in the bible, but because we sinfully allowed and allow it and did it. Some of the same forces have been at work in both racial subordination and discrimination against homosexuals.

So, when I speak of gender inclusive language, I am speaking of all the former considerations. Therefore, I advocate sermonic language which affirms women and men as partners in society. In such language lie the tools which help all of God's people to draw a bit closer to one another each day, as the Holy Spirit leads and directs our collective endeavors.

What, then, does it mean to be "*culturally inclusive*"? No one culture has been divinely ordained as superior to another culture. All have come short of the glory of God. But, The Compassionate One so loved us that the ultimate sacrifice was made for the redemption of all. Cultural inclusiveness is the recognition that diversity can be celebrated when it is not feared or dismissed as one more unnecessary act of political correctness. All cultures have great artists, laborers, humanitarians, professionals, and traditions. They also have biases, hateful and hurtful traditions, crooks, charlatans, and worse. Cultural inclusiveness demands that we understand and live as if we believe that The Ultimate One created an entire world with a variety of persons who have emerged with a variety of beliefs and traditions. One is not asked to agree with all the practices of another culture, but one must not degrade or reject the practices of another culture simply because that culture presents a different view of the world.

Herein, when I speak of cultural inclusiveness, I speak of the former considerations, coupled with the ultimate belief (lived and preached) that all persons of all cultures are divinely and wonderfully made and worthy of respect.

INCLUSIVENESS ISSUES

There are those for whom all this talk about inclusiveness is much ado about nothing. They are comfortable with exclusive language—"businessmen," "salesmen," "chairmen," etc., regardless of who is referenced. They find no fault in using "he" as a generic pronoun. For them, the norm is typically white or black, male, heterosexual, and middle class or wealthier. For others, talk of inclusiveness is labeled mere feminist hysteria and social propaganda by those with non-traditional family and social agendas. But, for those who would preach a faithful gospel that has its eye firmly fixed on the Beloved Community, inclusiveness is of critical importance.

Then, there is preaching that cements exclusion and sexism in the culture. This is done in numerous ways:

1. It is done by our refusal to broaden our moral imaginations, especially if to do so comes at a cost to us socially and or financially.

2. It is done by perpetuating cultural stereotypes: boys do not play with dolls; older women are spinsters; mothers smother children; women who date younger men are cougars; while older men who date younger women are just older men who date younger women; women are relational and men are problem solvers; women are domestic and men are hunter-gatherers. While some women may be domestic, so are some men, and some women are absolutely, not domestic. While some men may be hunter-gatherers, so are some women, and some men are absolutely not hunter-gatherers. Do not succumb to lazy generalities; work for inclusiveness.

3. It is done by non-parallel treatment of female and male subjects. For example,

Ladies' man (positive)	Man eater (negative)
Satyriasis (male equivalent of nymphomaniac)	and never used
Craftsmen	Crafts women (rarely used)
Alumni (correct term for male graduates)	Alumnae (correct term for women graduates and rarely used)
Army Wives	There is no male equivalent, so do not use the female term.
Prophet (male or female)	Prophetess (a word unnecessarily used to refer to female prophets)
Blonde (often used to refer to women of low intellect or as sex objects)	There is no male equivalent.
Brotherly love	There is no commonly used female equivalent.
Career woman	There is no male equivalent.
Concubine (refers only to women)[2]	Should only be used when giving specific scripture references.
Deacon (should refer to male and female deacons) unless the term concerns persons persons at various phases of licensing and ordination as clergy).	Deaconess (term for women deacons in some churches) and women who are not deacons, but are married to men who are deacons. Itinerant deacon is the term used mainly for non-paid women and men who serve in the African Methodist Episcopal, African Methodist Episcopal Zion, Christian Methodist Episcopal, the United Methodist Church, and perhaps other faith communities. This status is granted before these preachers are ordained and given

the title Elder. In the Episcopal and sectors of the Lutheran church, the term deaconess refers to women who are ordained for church work.

4. It is done by use of "ess" and "ette" words. Margaret Doyle, author of *The A-Z of Non-Sexist Language* writes:

> When added to perfectly acceptable, gender-neutral words like author, poet and manager, these [ess and ette] feminizing suffixes (along with '-trix', '-ine', and '-enne') contribute to a perception that the male is the standard form and the female is the subset. The use of -ess and -ette suffixes, in particular, suggests that the female is somehow less important than the male…. Not only are they disparaging and often facetious, but they are unnecessary. In most cases in which -ess and -ette endings are used, the gender of the person referred to is not important. If it is, it can be specified with a straightforward modifier: male author, female poet…. Generally, use the root form (author, poet, heir) of all these terms for both male and female; avoid the suffixes.[3]

Being inclusive is akin to being a good bible exegete. Good biblical exegetes preach what is in the text, not what they want to be there, need to find there; or, for lack of diligence, made up their minds was there. Good exegesis becomes a habit for those who are concerned with being "true" to biblical texts which are derived from certain contexts. Inclusiveness also becomes a habit, for those who are concerned with preaching a gospel that does not betray the *ultimate commandments* of the bible—that we *love God with all our hearts, souls, and minds, and our neighbor, as we love ourselves.*

Being gender inclusive in a sermon is not a sex issue; it is a justice issue. Cultural inclusiveness is also a matter of justice and love. Often, when preachers and many churches hear the term "inclusive," they immediately believe that what is to be discussed has to do with a person's gender. While this is likely a part of the discussion, the basic, bottom line is justice and love. Is it **just** for one sex to exclude the other from the work of God (and use sermons to do it)? Is that a **loving** thing to do? Is it **just** for one sex to declare that they are to have the leadership roles in the Church and society, and that others are to be subordinate? Is that a **loving** or **just** thing to do?

Cultural inclusiveness is often made an appendage of discussions on what is "politically correct," creating the expectation that justice is a superfluous discussion. However, given the plethora of sermons that continue to insult and exclude cultures, by resorting to stereotypical jokes and sermons that draw social boundaries in harsh attempts to keep certain cultures out, it is clear that many preachers still don't get the point about drawing in people with the Good News. We also continue to hear sermons that reek of anti-Semitism and homophobia, that expand patriarchy, and simply exclude persons. Cultural inclusiveness is more than being politically correct; it is doing justice.

There is no Good News without justice. There is no love, no peace, no community, without justice. And, there is no place for gospel preaching that portrays Jews as a "money hungry," "Jesus killing" group; or blacks as typically "criminal," "on welfare," "only achieving through affirmative action," etc.; or Latinos/a as "out to take American jobs" and "illegal;" or, Asians as a "closed group seeking to buy up as much American property as they can;" or God as only and always, or, primarily male. This is a simple lesson. Most people get it, except when it comes to giving up their own personal prejudices.

While many preachers are just clever enough not to say these exact things, their sermon examples and stories all too often convey these messages anyway. How often do we hear positive stories about black leaders other than during Black History Month? Who are the maids, soldiers, doctors, mechanics, bankers, lawyers, teachers, bus drivers, grocery store clerks, and leaders in our stories, and which professions do we honor? Why are so many of our sermon illustrations about white men or black men, never women? Why are so few of our positive stories about persons with limited formal educational training? Why are our heroes never people with physical or intellectual disabilities? Are most of our heroines and heroes old or all young? Do we disassociate with ease, from those media denounces as the new enemies, now Arabs and for some Latino/nas? We must do justice!

ANTI-SEMITISM AND ANTI-JUDAISM

Although it merits a much longer and more thorough treatment than this study guide will permit, I provide at least the following brief words about the continuing anti-Semitism that still pervades Christian churches. As were many Christians, I was taught anti-Semitism as a child. My well-meaning Sunday School teachers began my indoctrination by making sure that I knew that, according to the *bible*, the blood of Jesus was on the hands of Jews. Words such as anti-Semitism were not in their vocabulary, although they knew of the holocaust. They just wanted to make sure I knew who the *enemies* of Christ are.

Thank goodness that we do not have to stay where we start. We can pray, read, think, change, communicate with others, and love our way to truth, the whole truth which always has a context and sometimes a pretext. It was easy for me to accept, as a child, the culturally ready-made enemies of Christ laid out for me. However, hanging on to those embedded prejudices after I matured became my responsibility and my sin, if I did it.

Once I could read the bible and its history for myself, it was even easier to accept that the Jews are God's chosen because of promises made to their ancestors, and no amount of anti-Semitism or ignorance could change this fact that God declared throughout the Old Testament and even in the New Testament. In fact, I find it utterly amazing that we newcomers (non-Jews), who call ourselves the "chosen" of God, do not preach respectfully and accurately about our "chosen" foreparents. I am afraid that many of the embedded cultural biases that permeate the African American church and have become part of its accepted body of theological norms, are simply negative bequeaths that were handed down by white denominations and white theologians, too many of which have never been critically examined by some African American clergy. Preachers have a moral duty to analyze, expose, and excise such theology that is hurtful, and undermines the Beloved Community.

Anti-Semitism when perpetrated by whites, blacks, or anyone, is fed by centuries of wrong-thinking and deep-seated erroneous Church history and by the need of too many Christians to have a scapegoat or an enemy—someone to be against, as they charge forth as soldiers on the battlefield for the Lord. However, instead of someone to be against, with courage we can allow our moral imaginations to go instead in search of someone we can be for and stand with.

Thankfully, scholars have begun to push back hard against anti-Semitic preaching and teaching. Some include: Ronald J. Allen and Clark M. Williamson, who authored *Preaching the Gospels without Blaming the Jews: A Lectionary Commentary* and *Interpreting Difficult Texts: Anti-Judaism and Christian Preaching.* Howard Clark Kee and Irvin J. Borowsky edited the thoughtful book, *Removing Anti-Judaism from the Pulpit.* Ellis Rivkin has written *What Crucified Jesus?* Also see *Wayward Shepherds: Prejudice and the Protestant Clergy,* by Rodney Stark, Bruce D. Foster, Charles Y. Glock, and Harold E. Quinley.

HOMOPHOBIA

It is never good for the Church to be on the wrong side of right. Nevertheless, it happens. When it does, the resultant damage, destruction, harm, pain, and lingering sin can last for centuries. In some instances, the Church loses its moral and spiritual footing by condoning or taking specific actions that are antithetical to everything God and scripture have ordained. In other instances, it is the deadening silence of the Church, when unrelenting exhortation is called for, that causes the harm. All of this leads to exclusion not inclusion.

For example, we are still witnessing and suffering the ill effects of the American and European Church's decision to condone and justify enslavement of Africans. The harm caused by that one decision has had and continues to have enormous negative impacts around the world. The resulting negative toll this has had on generations of excluded Blacks is incalculable. The same is true for the Church's treatment of women. There is no way to determine the continuing damage to women and the losses suffered by the world generally because of the exclusionary policies employed against women by the Church. The Church's actions and silence, in both instances, have been rooted in scriptural justifications. Sermon after sermon has been used to institutionalize and maintain these exclusionary practices.

Currently, the Church is grappling with another major issue—homosexuality. Until now, almost uniformly, the Church's message to the homosexual community has been one of derisive negativity and exclusion. With little thought given to the effects that their exclusionary language and actions have on homosexuals, their children and other family members, and heterosexuals, clergy have preached sermon after sermon that contained mean, unforgiving, pronouncements for homosexuals.

My purpose for including this issue in the book is not to tell pastors and preachers what positions to take on homosexuality or any other subject. There, hopefully, each minister will be led by the Holy Spirit and his/her own moral and spiritual compass. Here, my goal is to challenge each pastor and preacher, when developing and delivering their sermons, to always be aware of contexts, effects, and purposes. In this vain, I believe all preachers have a duty to carefully study and exegete the bible before they reach hardened positions on sensitive subjects such as homosexuality.

First, we have a moral and theological obligation to explore related contextual issues. In this case: (a) gay bashing; (b) bullying of gay youth; (c) suicide by gay persons; (d) assaults and murdering of gay people because they are gay; (e) heterosexism and (f) current trends in science and social science regarding homosexuality. Otherwise, the body of our sermons may be rife with nothing more than uninformed, insensitive, homophobic ramblings. At the end of such sermons, there may be nothing to celebrate.

In a related but slightly different vein, preachers also have an obligation to consider the intended and likely effects of their sermons and the unintended consequences. Will someone who is homophobic feel justified in attacking or bullying a gay teen because the pastor railed against homosexuals? Will that gay teen be led to take his/her life after hearing your sermon, because he/she is convinced God has no place for him/her in the Church or heaven? Will the son or daughter of a homosexual parent leave your sermon more confused than when he/she entered the church? Will the parents of a homosexual child be made to feel it is their fault that their child is gay? Will your sermon leave some in the congregation wondering whether God made some huge mistake while forming creation?

Then, preachers have an obligation to seriously consider the purposes of each sermon they preach. Failure to do so will often lead to sermons that are bare of affirming principles, and unhelpful to those at whom the sermons are targeted. Whatever a preacher's ultimate position on homosexuality, each of his/her sermons on the subject should find a way to be thoughtful, inclusive, and loving.

Interestingly, in 2012, the Church (Protestant and Catholic) continues to spend an inordinate amount of time and energy denouncing homosexuality, mainly using two or three of what they believe are the nine references in the Bible concerning homosexuality. One has to wonder, with a list of issues plaguing communities that now include: murder, corporate greed, illiteracy, poverty, obesity, lack of affordable health care, dysfunctional families, domestic violence, rape, teen pregnancy, unemployment, suicide, mental illness, homelessness, racial profiling, racist lending practices, pedophilia, outsourcing of jobs, diseases, environmental racism, and classism (and I could go on and on and on) how does homosexuality even make the list of serious issues on which the Church regularly focuses?

However, many younger adults and some older adults are no longer willing to participate in helping[4] preachers blame homosexuals for the disintegration of families, and for the shattering of other social institutions and so-called norms. Not everyone is willing to accept the modern historical socialization that requires hatred or denigration of homosexuals. Such hate and denigration is just another way of further shattering the already fragile human family.

Recently, President Obama announced his evolved support of gay marriage. He indicated that it is a matter of civil rights and that current exclusions are divisive and wrong. Responding, many who in the past had staunchly supported civil rights for blacks, voiced vehement opposition to the President's stance. Numerous preachers who support President Obama, couched their opposition in this fashion: "He has to uphold the Constitution and push for equal rights for everyone. I answer to a different and higher authority. He can still be my President but we don't have to agree on everything." Those who already did not support President Obama, for many reasons, spewed the worst of the vitriol against homosexual equality and marriage.

Many who support the President, and many of those who do not, staunchly agree on their non-support of gay marriage. Both claim that their inability to support gay marriage is based upon their biblical beliefs. They are quick to say, "I can love the sinner, and hate the sin." Or, "It's not homosexuals that I am against, it's homosexual practice." They want to claim a "welcoming but not affirming" stance, to use the title of Stanley Grenz's book.

It is not necessary to detail all of the ways that the bible has been used to suppress, denigrate, and murder, women, Jews, Native Americans, and certainly African Americans. Though it is not altogether shocking, it is still disheartening, that some of the same people who have suffered most at the hands of biblical literalists and isegetes, would fall prey to the same misuse of scripture, when applied to the gay community. However, given the unhurried pace with which bigotry and oppression of groups has tended to be ameliorated in U.S. history, the acceptance of homosexuals and homosexuality has proceeded with lightning speed, since its designation as a disease in 1870. But, there is still so much to do be done.

Instead of concluding this section with a lengthy analysis of the 9 scriptures mentioned above, for those who are interested in re-considering their stance or at least want to hear all sides of the argument, I recommend the following books: (a) *Their Own Received Them Not: African American Lesbians and Gays in Black Churches* by Horace L. Griffin; (b) *The Good Book: Reading the Bible with Mind and Heart,* by Peter J. Gomes; (c) *Homosexuals and the Bible: Two Views* by Dan O. Via and Robert Gagnon; (d) *The History of Sexuality* (Volumes 1-3) by Michel Foucault; (e) *Mere Christianity* by C.S. Lewis; (f) *Sexuality and the Black*

Church: A Womanist Perspective by Kelly Brown Douglas; and, (g) *Embodiment and the New Shape of Black Theological Thought* by Anthony B. Pinn.

There are numerous additional books that can be helpful to those who are self-critical and self-questioning on the subjects of homophobia and the often related subject of heterosexism. Please read well beyond my short, suggested list. And more importantly, spend serious time in conversation with gay, lesbian, bisexual, and transgender men, women, and teens.

HOW TO BE INCLUSIVE

While some will declare that they are interested in being inclusive, they fear that it is too difficult and too awkward and that their church will judge them negatively, for being really inclusive. Even if it is difficult, it must be done. Even if your church fails to reward you for doing it, God will count you a success. And, remember, cultures do change. So do people, if enough work is done. For those who genuinely want to be gender and culturally inclusive, the following should prove helpful.

First, one must believe that all individuals are made in the image of The Wellspring of Life and stand equal before our Creator, regardless of gender, ethnicity, sexual preference, age, ability, or educational status. Each is part of Divine creation, and each has the need to be saved, loved, and encouraged. When preachers sincerely believe this in their head and heart, it is possible to move toward preparing sermons which bear this out and to start living it out. It is not enough to use inclusive language if one is not willing to live an inclusive lifestyle. If one does not believe that all persons have sacred worth and equal value, there is little or nothing that can be done that will bring this forth in one's preaching.

This is not to be confused with preaching a gospel that loves the person and hates their sin. While this is what should be done for all sins, all too often preachers use this notion as a cover to condemn behavior they abhor and to attack those sins that they and their congregation find convenient and easy to discuss. Sometimes, the abhorred behavior is detested by a particular preacher because that behavior connects with some deeply buried personal fear that the preacher has about himself or herself—some untouched and unresolved "thorn" in his or her side. In either case, this often leads to sermons based on a "class of particular sins" being preached.

This can typically be a function of the geographic regions in which persons live and of their denominational (faith community) allegiance. North Carolina Baptists, for example, do not preach against tobacco use as much as some. Prostitution, lying, stealing, drinking, and illegal drug use are favorite targets for some, while fornication, smoking, gambling, homosexuality, hanging out in nightclubs, and loose living (whatever that means—typically addressed as done by women) are the main sins for others. All are seeking an easy target to shoot down with fiery oratory. But people are best helped when inspired and persuaded to live as divine creations, not when they are attacked, frightened, scolded, or shamed.

Interestingly enough, one is not likely to hear overweight preachers preach about gluttony or care of the body as the Temple of God; or preachers who cheat on their spouses preach on adultery, although they may preach against fornication and homosexuality; or, preachers in wealthy congregations preach about the "love of money as the root of all evil." Preachers with congregations in areas that are filled with military bases and military families are not likely to preach much against the evils of war. And, we are all aware of sermons that place the ideologies of one political party over another, as preachers seek to identify with their congregations and express their own (the preacher's) political ideologies.

After preachers believe that all persons have sacred worth, they then need to know that they do not have to have mastered Greek, Hebrew, and Aramaic to be gender inclusive, and certainly not to be culturally inclusive. Some tools that are helpful are a lexicon and a concordance that contain a Hebrew, Aramaic, and Greek dictionary. A lexicon displays the verses in a text in the original language on one side of the page, and then translates those words into English on the other side of the page. While biblical scholars will all agree that there are some Greek, Hebrew, and Aramaic words for which there are no really good equivalents in English, in most instances this is not the case.

A lexicon will enable preachers to see that often enough what we claim as the unadulterated gospel is no more than translations preferred by men of certain social classes who had particular agendas. For example, consider the use of the word "man." If one looks in a *Strong's Concordance*, he or she will find the word man listed about 4,000 times! It is possible to simply accept *Strong's* listing and move on. However, consider what Nancy Hardesty has revealed in her book *Inclusive Language in the Church*:

> . . . Citations for the term man take up twenty-two columns on the huge pages of my *Strong's Exhaustive Concordance*, and citations of men cover another fourteen columns. Each column includes 116 citations. This means that a woman reading an English Bible finds the words man or men more than four thousand times!

> In Greek, however the writers carefully made a distinction between anthropos, which means human, person, people and humanity, and aner, which means adult male and/or husband. The New Testament authors used anthropos predominantly. They were careful to use anthropos when speaking about people in general, a fact that is lost on English readers because translators have invariably rendered it "man" and "men."[6]

In addition to using a lexicon, concordance, and proper dictionaries, those who would be inclusive must be mindful that, as I discussed earlier, there are many biblical translations. It is best to use version(s) that most help congregations understand the bible and its culture in depth, along with strong lexicons, concordances, and commentaries. Some use the Inclusive Language Lectionary, and many use a combination of translations to arrive at the most reliable meanings of texts.

Additionally, remember that language is always spoken in a context. Language that may be acceptable to one congregation may be offensive to another. Words can sometimes even take on different meaning by geographical region and certainly along cultural lines. There is also a comfort level to be considered relative to context. While a discussion of Jesus coming forth from the "womb" of Mary, and the mention of a woman's "menstrual cycle," "menopause," or "erectile dysfunction" would not be noticed in some congregations, others will find such language quite uncomfortable. Some congregations are comfortable with terms such as gay, queer, homosexual, transgender, and lesbian. Some congregations are only comfortable if such terms are used in discussing sinful lifestyles. Although there are times when one is called to make the comfortable uncomfortable, this should be done with much prayer and great care.

Of great importance, for this discussion, is the need for all preachers to begin to ask more questions, as they approach a pericope. This is thoroughly discussed in Chapter 5. Isn't it interesting how many of the prostitutes in the bible are also heroines? Why is it that when angels appear before most men in the bible, the men faint or have to be told not to fear? When they appear before women, a dialogue immediately begins. How did the fish in the Jonah story become a whale? How did we come to talk about the fruit in the Garden as an apple? How did we come to talk about there being three Wise Men? Why do we presume shepherds are male, when Rachel (Genesis 29) and other women tended sheep? If God is a spirit, and we can choose to talk of God as our Heavenly Father who is a Spirit, could we not speak of God as our Heavenly Mother, who is a spirit? Does God become weak if she is referred to as female? Are men stronger than women? If so, in what ways, and in what circumstances? Does it matter? Who makes this decision, and why are certain characteristics chosen as indicators of strength and not others? Why is the word spirit (which is gender neutral) referred to as he and not she when we want to make clear that the Spirit is not a thing?

Further, because preaching is a form of verbal communication, it is extremely important to take care to avoid awkward words and phrases such as "Godself" in order to avoid saying "herself" or "himself." It is wise not to stray very far from accepted English speech patterns, even while being intentionally inclusive. This can be done with very little effort; it simply takes practice.

Care also must be taken to avoid overkill. Consider the following example of the use of the word "God," to avoid using "he": "Grace is a gift from God because God is the giver of all good and perfect gifts. Our God is greatly to be praised and thanked for all that our God has done. Praise be to God for the great things that God has done."

On the other hand, as one ventures into the world of inclusiveness, DO NOT let fear of making a mistake or seeming clumsy stop you. This won't be the first or the last time that you as a preacher say something about which you feel awkward. If you must err, do so on the side of inclusiveness. Err on the side of justice, and on the side of love. Even if it feels awkward at first; in time, it will not and you will not. Begin with a list of five or six words that you constantly use that you know are not inclusive and make them inclusive. Then, just continue adding to your list.

As a child, I was taught that a name for God is *The Awesome One*. How fitting. But, The Awesome One has numerous names. Use more than one or two of them; and as pastor, preacher, and teacher, teach students and congregations to do the same. It is a truism that *where preachers lead in love and loyalty, the people follow*. Once a congregation trusts a pastor, that person can do a great deal to remove sexist, elitist, racist, and homophobic language and behavior from a congregation. And, believe it or not, most people want to grow and be more inclusive; give them opportunities to do so.

While there can be male references used to describe The Upholder of the Weak, they should be balanced with female references. It is especially important to teach this to clergy who are training by watching you; and, to parishioners who read scripture and teach in the church. The pastor cannot be the only one who pushes for inclusive language, if a church is expected to grow in this area, but the pastor must lead the way for the entire congregation.

One can speak of The Binder of Wounds and never offend, all the while giving listeners new ways to think about The Divine. One can replace the characters in stories with non-traditional models, not stereotypes, and new names, and gain an attentive hearing from congregations. Some will know that something different is happening and will welcome the change. Others will know that something which feels unpleasant is happening to them, but they will puzzle at how they can fight it and, hopefully, will wonder why they want to fight it.

A male Korean preacher told the following story to a congregation in a rural town:

> After we had been in the air a few hours, the ride started to get really bumpy. As the captain spoke to us, she said those words that all of us who hate to fly dread: "Ladies and gentlemen, we are experiencing some severe turbulence." At this point, my eyes were immediately directed to the

phones they now have on airplanes. I pulled out one and called my office. My assistant informed me that all was well, but he was quite tired having been up all night with a sick child.

He went on to say that the Governor had passed into legislation a bill to provide more money for homeless shelters and this would help our shelter collaboration project. As I hung up the phone, a flight attendant came by and said that I looked familiar. It quickly dawned on me that he and his family used to live near my family where I grew up. We reminisced throughout the flight and, as I prepared to change planes, another passenger commented how awful the weather was and how bumpy the flight had been. I was so busy celebrating a victory for the less fortunate and catching up with an old friend, I had forgotten all about the rough flight and my fear of flying. God knew what I needed to calm my nerves.

Tools such as the Inclusive Language Lectionary, the Book of Common Prayer of the Episcopal Church, several of the inclusive aids for worship produced by the United Methodist Church, and other tools that can be found at any major religious bookstore, and all over the Web, will also greatly aid in your quest to be inclusive.

Finally, preachers would do well to note that worship is a complete experience, and a sermon that is inclusive may be half heard, or not heard at all, if it is preceded or followed by other acts of worship (singing, extending hospitality, praying, scripture reading, etc.) that are not inclusive. Make your entire worship service inclusive. In meetings with all who will lead in worship, explain that your church is to show love, justice, inclusiveness, and the heart of Christ at all times, in all things. Then, follow with examples of how this **is** shown and how it is **not** shown.

As a closing note, it is likely that preachers, especially pastors, will be more inclusive, if they do so with intentionality. Such intention will be learned and practiced by their congregations.

Reverend Nolan Williams Jr., a liturgist for The African American Lectionary, shared the following ideas in the "Who So Ever Will" 2011 worship unit that was featured in The African American Lectionary:

(1) Even if you perceive yourself to be a welcoming congregation, do not assume you are. Do a hospitality assessment:

- Have a stranger visit your congregation and tell you what he/she sees, hears, feels.
- Take a hospitality assessment of your congregation at:
  http://archive.elca.org/evangelizingChurch/congregations

(2) Identify everyone in the congregation as members of the "Welcoming Team":

- Provide intentional training for congregational members throughout the year on anti-racism, interacting with persons with disabilities, persons from other ethnic backgrounds, women, gays, lesbians, and transgender people.
- Periodically include a short public "Affirmation of Welcome" in worship.
- Graciously ask that no one have a "reserved" pew or seat except persons with disabilities for whom certain seating may be necessary.[7]

NOTES

1. Peter J. Gomes, *The Good Book: Reading the Bible with Mind and Heart* (New York, NY: William Morrow and Company, Inc., 1996), 99–100.

2. Margaret Doyle, *The A–Z of Non-Sexist Language* (London: The Women's Press, 1995).

3. Ibid., 26–27.

4. Half of Americans Support Gay Marriage in New Gallup Poll http://usnews.nbcnews.com/news/2012/05/08/11603182-half-of-americans-support-gay-marriage-in-new-gallup-poll?lite

5. Paul Rabinow, ed. *The Foucault Reader* (New York, NY: Patheon Books, 1984), 322.

6. Nancy A. Hardesty, *Inclusive Language in the Church* (Atlanta: John Knox Press, 1987), 80.

7. See the entire unit online at http://www.theafricanamericanlectionary.org/PopupWorshipAid.asp?LRID=225

A VEHICLE FOR INCLUSIVENESS

1. Begin by praying that the Holy Spirit will help you overcome any personal biases or prejudices that you have, and will allow you to view all persons as created in God's Divine image.

2. Select a pericope and a text. Read the text in several bible translations.

3. Then read your text in a lexicon, using a concordance, a dictionary, and good commentaries. Afterwards, write or type your text. Determine if there are instances where Greek, Hebrew, or Aramaic words are difficult to translate into English. It may take two or three English words to translate one Greek word. In translating, always err on the side of inclusiveness.

4. Relative to being inclusive, there are three questions to pose throughout the development of your sermon, especially after you have completed a first draft:

> **Q1:** What personal bias do I bring to this text? Bias includes gender and cultural biases. Also, do not assume that any group, gender, or bible character is incapable of bias.

> **Q2:** Does my use of this text in any way slight or degrade any culture or gender?

> **Q3:** Have I earnestly used this text, my sermon illustrations, songs, or examples to help listeners view all persons as equals?

5. After your first draft is written, list all instances of gender bias and cultural bias that you detect in your draft. Make the appropriate changes to cure the bias problems.

6. Re-read your draft and identify any awkward words or phrases that you have used in an attempt to be inclusive. Make the desired changes to relieve some of the awkwardness.

_____

_____

_____

_____

_____

_____

_____

_____

_____

_____

_____

_____

7. Identify how many times you referred to God as "he." Then, insert other names for God that are either non-gendered and or that give God more than a male gender.

Male References for the word God	New References

8. Read your sermon draft to detect how many times you have used the **same words** repeatedly to describe commonly used religious language, such as God, Holy Spirit, Jesus, Church, etc. (Remember, there are more than 90 names for the Church in the New Testament, and more than 75 names for Jesus in the Old and New Testaments, combined.) List the words you used that need to be changed. Store this list in a file or on CD for future review.

Words Commonly Used	New Words

9. After you complete a first draft or an outline, check for instances of racist stereotypes, anti-Semitism, and homophobia. Especially pay attention to your illustrations and examples. List all examples of racist stereotypes, anti-Semitism, and homophobia. Make the necessary changes.

_____

_____

_____

_____

_____

_____

_____

_____

_____

9

SERMON CELEBRATIONS AND SERMON CONCLUSIONS

Two of the most neglected areas of sermon preparation are the sermon celebration and the sermon conclusion. First, the sermon celebration. The sermon celebration is extremely important in any congregation since the celebration is the climactic effort to move hearers so that they remember the text and its influence is later reflected in their behavior. The same is true of the sermon conclusion. Below are the characteristics and materials appropriate to celebration. Sermon conclusions will then be discussed.

There are eight important characteristics of a sermon celebration:

1. Celebration is affirmative.

That it is affirmative is the most important characteristic of a celebration. In grammatical terms, its verbs are in the indicative mood and its sentences are declarative. People are moved to be glad about what is, as opposed to what is not; what is right, as opposed to what is wrong; what is possible, as opposed to what is impossible. The celebration demands that the preacher be true to the gospel as *good* news.

2. Celebration is NOT admonition or challenge.

The behavioral aim of the sermon may clearly require that one admonish, even rebuke at times. But this cannot be considered cause for celebration. People do not generally rejoice over what they are *supposed* to do. Rather, the major emotional identifications and behavioral changes are expected to occur in the *transforming* moment of the celebration of what God has done in Christ, and what we can do through Christ who strengthens us.

The prophetic criticisms, rebukes, and the like belong in the body of the sermon. This does not mean that a good celebration is "soft on sin"; it simply means that admonitions and rebukes belong earlier in the sermon. The celebration itself is a major tactic against sin, in that it transforms and empowers hearers to follow the Word and will of God. This means that imperative words such as "ought" and "should" are not for the celebration—neither are conditional words such as "if" and "when." They are reserved for earlier in the sermon. Additionally, imperative sentences are direct admonition, and conditional sentences are veiled or indirect admonition.

There are some phrases commonly used in preaching that never belong in the celebration: "The trouble with us is . . ."; or, "You know, some people are just like that." These are not good celebratory statements. In fact, they are also weak, when used to admonish. They declare the obvious and amount to cheap attempts at audience response and/or are based on judgmental shots at "those other people."

The **penetrating question** that amounts to a challenge is not celebration either. Occasionally, a sermon will end with a challenge placed in the form of a penetrating question. However, when this happens it should be intentional, instead of a celebration that went wrong. More is said below about the use of this rhetorical device.

3. Celebration is the point of highest emotional intensity in a sermon.

Since the sermon involves an experiential, holistic encounter with biblical truth, the peak of the experience must be expressed holistically. While there is emotional impact throughout the sermon, the celebration is the peak of purposeful emotion. Not only does celebration require heightened rhetoric, but celebration also requires peaks in tone and dramatic intensity. This does not necessarily mean a higher level of sound or decibel output, but it is the peak of the preacher's personal identification with the message.

The contagion of celebration begins with the sincere conviction and joy of the preacher. God uses the witness of the preacher's joy, both spoken and embodied, to stir up the focused affirmation and rejoicing of the congregation. God also uses the joyous witness of responsive laity during the celebration period.

4. Celebration is drawn from the sermon text, whenever possible.

The first step in developing a celebration is to focus on the text of the sermon, seeking any material that already suggests the basis for a celebration. If there is none, then look in the larger pericope, if the text came out of a larger pericope. If there is none in either place, then look in another biblical passage or other resource for a way to celebrate in a manner that focuses on and supports the behavioral aim of the sermon and melds well with the main text.

5. Celebration flows smoothly from the main body of the sermon.

The ideal celebration will flow smoothly from the last point of the sermon, maintaining sermon focus and applicability to the behavioral aim and text throughout. When this does not happen, review the transition sentence that took you from the last sub-point in your outline to the celebration. Make sure that there is not a sharp break. That is, avoid the use of celebrations which cannot be made to flow from the rest of the sermon—those that are "tacked on" the body of the sermon. This mainly refers to stock clichés that are over-used and seldom, if ever, related to the behavioral aim of the sermon.

Some preachers have been taught that every sermon should end at the cross. Of course, this is a great way to celebrate, if the sermon **naturally** flows to the cross and the resurrection. But, your sermons may not have anything to do with any aspect of the crucifixion or the resurrection; and, so cannot flow there. Do not force a text to flow in a direction in which it was never intended to flow. This is what is meant by failing to preach with exegetical and homiletical integrity. Always be sure to respect the text.

6. Celebration occurs only once.

Make sure that there is no more than one celebration. One frequent reason sermons have two celebrations is the failure to narrow the behavioral aim to one, well-defined aim. Another is the misguided effort to achieve a better audience response. It must be borne in mind, however, that when sermons have more than one concluding peak, only the last one will most likely be remembered. Multiple celebrations are also likely to lead the hearer's mind away from the original text and behavioral aim the preacher actually had in mind for the sermon; and, thus, serve as an eraser on the main value of the sermon. This is true because most second and third celebrations occur because the first one, which was the correct one (though perhaps, not delivered well), in the preacher's estimation, failed to generate the appropriate or desired response in the congregation.

Related to this problem is the need to avoid more than one thing about which to celebrate. If in fact you have two or more things/issues about which you celebrate, this is a clear sign that the behavioral aim was **too broad** in the first place; or, that one didn't follow the aim with which one began. In some cases, it may even mean that one is introducing new information and aims instead of celebrating and concluding. **Never introduce new information or suggest new solutions in the celebration**. Celebrate the achievement of one behavioral aim, once and be seated!

7. Celebration is a peak experience, not a summary of points previously stated.

Good celebrations are intentionally focused emotionally, so that the feelings of preacher and congregation reach their peak in the celebration. These feelings are **ecstatic reinforcement of the text and behavioral aim**. If one is tied to the traditional idea that celebrations must also summarize, it is good to remember that the sermon text and behavioral aim do, in fact, sum up the points (moves) in a sermon. Moves, as such, should **not** be actually reiterated in the celebration, especially since they were not designed to serve primarily celebratory purposes. They were designed for the body of the sermon.

8. Celebration is characterized by intensity of emotion, not by sound volume.

There is a widespread misconception, especially in sectors of African American faith communities and other ethnic communities with styles similar to those of these African American faith communities, that loudness equals celebration. Increased volume could, in fact, mean the opposite; or, anger and hostility. Intensity is as easily achieved with whispers as with shouts and well-placed pauses and silence. It depends on sincerity, the context, and the content of the celebration. A declaration of sorrow or commitment is seldom shouted, but it may be very effective in softer tones, especially in cultural groups where preaching loudly is frowned upon. In some African cultures, a raised voice is a sign of anger. Good celebration is purposefully intense and focused emotion at whatever level of sound output.

EXAMPLE FOR DEVELOPING A SERMON CELEBRATION

The following sermon celebration outline comes from the Old Testament narrative concerning Queen Esther. The text is Esther 4:14c: "...*who knoweth whether thou art come to the kingdom for such a time as this?*" The behavioral aim is to move oppressed persons to acts of liberation, trusting that they will be used to make a difference.

This story has a happy ending, but does not have specific words or phrases that lend to a celebration, lifting the purpose of God-given vocation. This purpose or aim is clearly exemplified in the courage and devotion of Esther. The challenge, then, is to design a celebration that lifts Esther and lifts acts of liberation and trust at the same time. Elements for celebration are in chapters 8 and 9 of the book of Esther, describing the feasts and gladness of joy of the Jews. But, none of these feasts praise Esther; the glory seems to all fall to Mordecai, her kinsman, who calls her to action.

The celebration proposed here, then, must go beyond Esther to more recently oppressed people who have answered God's call to make a difference. One could use any historic list with which his or her congregation will relate. My list included Harriett Tubman, Sojourner Truth, Fannie Lou Hamer, and Barbara Jordan. I used women since Esther is a woman.

Celebration Focus Topic Sentence: God continues to bless those who honor God's call.

Sub¶ a: Topic Sentence: The Jews are saved and God keeps calling folk.

Sub¶ b: Topic Sentence: God calls people in our time to work and blessings and to blessings in the hereafter.

CONCLUSIONS

Yes, a celebration is a conclusion. However, not all conclusions are celebrations, on purpose. Some religious contexts have little or no understanding of sermon celebration. In these contexts, preachers simply want to conclude a sermon well. In such cases, there are several mistakes to avoid:

1. Do not fail to finish strong. Some preachers fail to give adequate attention to how they will conclude, and the result can be a limp or a whimper of a conclusion. Always finish strong, and remain faithful to the behavioral aim of your sermon.

2. Avoid histrionics, if you preached a weak sermon. If one has preached a weak sermon, all of the histrionics in the world at the point of the conclusion will not help. If anything, histrionics will make the preacher seem desperate. The best thing to do is sit down quickly and quietly.

3. Do not go to the cross, unless your text and sermon clearly take you there. Going to the cross to conclude is a staple in some preaching traditions. This is problematic, because so many texts cannot be connected to Calvary, without almost twisting the preacher and the texts in knots. If this is a tradition in your faith community, break with tradition! Remain true to the text and good exegesis.

4. Do not fail to take a good exit, when you have one, especially when you only do so to get a bigger congregational reaction. After you have concluded, there is no need for your personal testimony, tear-jerking comments concerning a difficult time in your life, or a very personal story that makes people believe you are a transparent preacher. While each of these may heighten the preaching moment, they may also kill it if the audience clearly knows that you should have stopped sooner and you did not.

Multiple conclusions usually occur after the first one has failed to achieve what the preacher believed was adequate response. This means the second or third try is likely to concern another behavioral aim altogether. This is tragic, since the last conclusion will most likely be the one best remembered. Good preaching maintains the integrity of the chosen behavioral aim, leaving the rest to the Holy Spirit. Do not get so distracted by a desired response that you forget your original intention for preaching the sermon.

5. Avoid conclusions that contain too much. If your conclusion contains songs, poetry, and a story, it contains too much! If you decide to conclude with a song, use only one song; do not try to mix the lyrics of two songs. The same applies to poems. Finally, if you are concluding with an illustration, use only one. That is sufficient.

6. Avoid concluding by quoting numerous scriptures that are disconnected from the overall aim of the sermon and your text. This is absolutely the wrong thing to do.

7. Do not attempt to meld texts in the conclusion; do so in the sermon. In a sermon that uses multiple texts, such as an Old Testament text, a Psalm, and more than one Gospel reading, by the point of the conclusion and **not** during the conclusion, one must meld all texts in a cohesive fashion. It is difficult to

take multiple texts and bring them together in a sermonically interesting and exegetically legitimate fashion. However, the conclusion is not the place to "tie up all lose ends." It is the point in which all is settled and one finishes with final words that give prominence to, in some fashion, the main aim that the preacher had in delivering the sermon to a particular congregation at a particular moment in history.

CONCLUDING WITH A CHALLENGE

I am not an advocate of concluding the average sermon with a challenge. This is likely due to the fact that given their social location, those to whom I most often preach rarely need additional challenges. The lives of these hearers are daily filled with challenges. More and more, my sense is that this is true for most communities, regardless of ethnicity and social location. However, at some point, on some issue, regardless of one's gender, social location, and audience, one will have to conclude a sermon with a challenge. Following are considerations when doing so:

1. Do not devolve into a challenge. One must be intentional, when concluding with a challenge. One should not end up challenging a congregation because his or her sermon devolved into a challenge.

2. Make sure you have given answers and "how to" information before you conclude by challenging a congregation. Do not challenge a congregation without also giving them answers and methods on how to solve the problems. This is a common preaching mistake. Preachers will name problem after problem or sin after sin. Meanwhile, listeners sit waiting for answers. Listeners may even realize they are guilty of each sin named; but, what they need are ways to stop sinning or ways to avoid the sins. Tell people how to love more, pray more, repent faster, become advocates for others, take responsibility for their own faith journeys, read the bible, and you know what else belongs on this very long list. So, issue the challenge, yes; but make sure you have offered appropriate solutions, even if the solution is just to have folk live with the tension of their state of affairs; or, accept that the preacher does not have a solution to their predicament.

3. To challenge a congregation is not to belittle or insult it. Yes, there are times when one has to afflict the comfortable, but preaching with a pastor's heart (even if one is not the pastor of the congregation to whom he or she is preaching) reminds preachers that, even when we are doling out harsh medicine, it need not be rammed down the throat of anyone to whom we preach. Also, never offer a challenge out of anger, especially when your anger is pointed at your congregation, denomination, or those who want to see you fail. One can conclude in righteous indignation but never anger.

4. Make sure you are up to meeting the challenge(s) you lay before others. Even when we are correct in challenging a congregation, our words will fall on deaf ears or even be heard with contempt if the life we live is in opposition to the challenges we lift for others. I am always reminded of this when I hear preachers who are financially rich, due to their snookering and robbing of the poor challenge people to give more to the Church or a particular ministry for the poor; or, when I hear preachers who are abusive within their households challenge others to be more forgiving and loving. If it is known or not known that you have a problem in the sermonic area of focus, acknowledge (without oversharing personal details), that this is a "growing edge" for you too. If you have overcome a particular problem, you can also share this without suggesting that others will do it the way you did it; or, in the time-frame in which you did it.

5. A challenge must be theologically grounded in the Word of God. More and more, though this is not a new historic occurrence, preachers "carry the water" for their personal (not always God's) stances on social issues, for politicians, and even conglomerates. Always be aware of your reasons for presenting the

challenges you do; and, make sure that those reasons are theologically grounded in the Word of God and not elsewhere.

6. Your conclusion should not contain new information, concepts, recommendations, or answers that were not provided in the body of the sermon. Again, it is the conclusion. So, avoid the tendency to mention an issue that crossed your mind in the excitement or lethargy of the moment. Also, avoid trying to make clearer any concepts or definitions that you have a sense were not made clear earlier in the sermon.

CONCLUDING WITH A PENETRATING QUESTION

A question is a familiar device for issuing challenges: "Peter do you love me? . . . Then, feed my sheep." "What would it profit a person to gain the whole world and lose his or her soul?" Its familiar use, as a device for issuing a challenge is one reason that the penetrating question can be a formidable rhetorical device with which to conclude a sermon, especially if you can couch the question within a captivating story. The following example of concluding a sermon with a penetrating question is from Dr. Fred Craddock. As a setup for the remarks below, in the body of the sermon, Dr. Craddock aimed to persuade us to care more for others, so that they would come to believe in the Church as an entity of hospitality and compassion for everyone. He began the sermon by telling us the story of a woman, who showed up right after the service, at a church he was pastoring. Now, his conclusion:

> As I stood at the back of a church that woman said again, to me, "I don't believe that there are people in the church who care. I just don't believe that." In an instant, my mind went back to my father, when he lay in a hospital room, covered with clear tubes in every place that they could put one and there were cords, cords, everywhere.
>
> My father had never liked the Church or church people, for that matter. He believed that they were out to con you. He never wanted to talk about religion and that kind of stuff. But, when my father was hospitalized, the people from my church came to visit, and brought gifts, and food and made calls and prayed for him day in and day out. Finally, one day he turned in bed and said to me, "You know, I was wrong about those church people. I was wrong; they do care." As I returned my attention to the woman, she exclaimed, "If there are people in the Church who really care, show these people to me. Who are they? Show them to me." Can I give her your name? Can I give her your name?

A VEHICLE FOR DEVELOPING CELEBRATIONS AND CONCLUSIONS

Reviewing a Celebration

1. After you have completed your first draft, review your celebration to ensure that it is affirmative and concerns your behavioral aim. (Are you being glad that this aim was accomplished in some form?)

2. Check to make sure that you have not subtly or unknowingly inserted some exhortation or admonition in your celebration. Watch for words such as "challenge," "must," "ought," "if," and "when." Delete and/or rewrite as necessary.

3. Check to make sure that the flow from the main body of your sermon to the celebration is smooth. Look for abrupt shifts in thought, from the end of the body of the sermon to the celebration.

4. If you are using a hymn in the celebration, make sure that the hymn **concerns** the text(s) and your behavioral aim, not just includes a word or phrase that is in the text.

5. Check to see if you could have drawn your celebration from the text(s) and did not. If so, make the great sacrifice and start over on your celebration.

6. If your celebration could not come from the text(s), check to make certain that whatever you chose as celebration material, reflects positively on the same issue that is raised by your text(s).

7. Check to make sure you only have **ONE** celebration.

8. Check to make sure you did not mix the lyrics of multiple songs or the words of multiple poems; or, give multiple illustrations in your conclusion.

9. Check to make sure you did not reiterate your moves (points) in your celebration.

Reviewing a Conclusion

1. Practice your conclusion aloud. Make sure your voice does not trail off, when giving it. Finish strong.

2. Check your sermon to make sure have not unnecessarily mentioned the cross, and or the resurrection, if they are not tightly connected to your text and behavioral aim.

3. Check to make sure you only have **ONE** conclusion.

4. Is your conclusion to the point—meaning, is it tightly written and does not include too much? For example, see if you have a song and a poem or a song and an illustration; that is too much. Have you concluded with verses from more than one song? If so, rearrange the conclusion, so that only one song is needed.

5. Did you include numerous scriptures in your conclusion? If so, pare down the number of scriptures. Choose one or two that clearly but concisely make your point.

6. If you preached from a lectionary, do not conclude by attempting to thread together all of your texts; do that in the body of the sermon.

Reviewing a Concluding Challenge

1. If you are concluding with a challenge, be intentional about doing so.

2. Check to make sure that you have not put forth challenges for which you did not offer solutions earlier in the sermon.

3. Check the language of your challenge. Is it insulting or belittling to hearers?

4. Remember, people are more persuaded by seeing examples of godly behavior by preachers than they are by preachers who challenge listeners to do what the preacher does not do; or, at least state it as a "growing edge."

5. Check your conclusion to make sure it is grounded in the Word of God and not in your personal views or views you advocate on behalf of others.

6. Make sure your challenge does not contain **new** information, concepts, or recommendations that you did not mention in some way in the body of the sermon.

Reviewing Concluding with a Penetrating Question

Develop a penetrating question with which to conclude your sermon. Make sure that you can answer the following questions affirmatively.

- Does your sermon build to your penetrating question?
- Is your penetrating question an outgrowth of your behavioral aim?
- Is your penetrating question brief—no more than one short sentence?
- Does your penetrating question require action, not just thought, on the part of hearers?
- Is your penetrating question compelling?

10

SUMMING IT ALL UP

Now that you have reached the end of the study guide, you can see that the process that leads to good preaching is detailed and lengthy. As I said previously, the process gets easier and moves along quicker, as you engage the process. This engagement will require that you review each of your sermons before and after you preach them, to keep honing your skills. Concentrate on your weaknesses and then strengthen those things that you already do well. Most importantly, do not attempt to take shortcuts. It will show in your preaching, if you do.

Accept that the mechanics of preaching have changed. You do not need to and should not embrace all of the changes, but you should absolutely be aware of their existence and what this means for you as a preacher. Take seriously the call to develop behavioral aims that are grounded in mutuality and solidarity. Write your behavioral aim at the top of your outline and or each page of your sermon, to keep you focused on it.

Always be purposeful about preaching holistically and including details that make a sermon come alive. Understand the genre of your sermon and do the long and difficult work of exegesis—all of it. Do not attempt to take exegetical shortcuts. Write and rewrite your sermon until it is focused and balanced. Quite importantly, always be inclusive in your preaching and conclude or celebrate well!

PULPIT AND PREACHING ETIQUETTE

It is time to preach. There are basic rules of pulpit etiquette that should be employed. The following are some rules of pulpit etiquette, when one is not the pastor at the church, where he or she will preach.

Centering Yourself and Prayer
Hopefully, you are well-rested. Adequate rest and regular exercise are necessary, if you want to consistently preach well, especially if you want to approach the preaching moment with optimum energy. If you are not well-rested, as much as possible, calm and center yourself before you preach, and be sure that you have prayed prior to the preaching moment. In most churches, it is acceptable to kneel and pray, as one enters a pulpit. It is also acceptable to give a **short** prayer before one begins to preach. A long prayer is totally inappropriate, at this point. Your prayer should only concern your desire that the Holy Spirit be present during the preaching moment and the receptiveness of those who will receive the Word.

Reviewing Your Manuscript
It is fine to glance at your manuscript before you stand to preach. However, do not do this for a long period of time or in a way that takes you out of the worship experience.

Securing Your Manuscript

If using a manuscript, make sure that it is contained within a folder or binder that will absolutely not allow sheets of your manuscript to fly off the pulpit or get out of order. Legion are the stories of flying manuscripts and preachers losing their place while preaching because they somehow caused pages of their manuscript to get out of order. Further, do not forget to sequentially number the pages of your sermon. That will make reordering them easier if they become disarranged.

Also, make sure that you can easily locate your scripture if you are reading it from a bible. It is not the best thing for a congregation to watch a preacher turn page after page hunting for his or her scripture passage, especially when multiple scriptures from different areas of the bible are being read. Place a long bookmark(s) in your bible and that will solve the problem. If using a Blackberry or tablet, be sure that your device is properly charged and ready for you to begin reading when you wish to do so.

Pulpit Attire

Much has changed in the area of pulpit attire. Many guest preachers now mainly preach in suits, not robes; and, some women preach in pantsuits. If you are not at your home church, and even if you are, and have not preached there in a while, and especially if the church has a new pastor, ask what is the preferred attire. Typically, congregations prefer robes during special days on their church calendar and during certain seasons of the church year. Again, ask what is the preference, especially, if the church is without a pastor.

Be sure that your attire is comfortable for preaching. Comfortable attire begins with wearing the right shoes. This is not the time for brand new shoes that have not been broken in, nor is it the time for very high heels, as they may become uncomfortable, if a preacher stands for more than 20 minutes. Men should also pay attention to neckties and make sure that they are loose and comfortable, and they should avoid bowties that are not secure. Of course, men and women should avoid tight-fitting clothing.

Now, on to more delicate aspects of pulpit attire. Every individual has his or her own style of dress. Some are more comfortable with dark colors; and, overall for them, less of everything is more. Others tend toward loud colors, large jewelry, and even bright makeup. Here are some safe rules of thumb: For men, after one gets past a dark beige suit (unless asked to wear white), he has gone far enough on the color spectrum. The top five male pulpit colors are still black, navy blue, brown, gray, and dark beige. For women, the same five colors are the safest. However, it is not necessary for women to avoid bright colors altogether, especially if they are paired with a dark color—for instance, a gold jacket with a black skirt, or a teal jacket with a navy blue skirt.

Flowery colorful outfits for women and flowery shirts and ties for men are typically problematic and can distract from the message being heard. Then there is the matter of lengths at which women should wear skirts and dresses. The rule of thumb is that a skirt or dress that is above the knee when one is seated, is probably too short. I have often seen women place what are called lap scarves over their knees to ensure that they are not accused of revealing too much. I suggest that instead of a lap scarf, which gives the appearance that you wore a skirt or dress that is too short, just select a garment of the right length for you before you leave home.

Two final attire notes: One, always be mindful of the amount of jewelry that is worn. For men, a watch, a bracelet, and two rings are more than enough. For women, avoid long earrings. Also, two rings, a bracelet (not one that is large or that hangs), and a simple watch, not one that dangles, are sufficient.

Two, prepare for the temperature of the church, before and after you preach. Some churches will be extremely hot. This can affect your throat. Be well-hydrated. Avoid cough drops that are not specifically intended to clear the throat. Heat can, of course, affect the extent to which you perspire, so always carry a handkerchief and be prepared to change clothes, if necessary, after you finish preaching. This will require that you carry a garment bag.

Churches can also be very cold. There are no easy answers here, as it is rarely possible for air conditioning to be shut off without making the worship experience uncomfortable for the congregation. It is acceptable to ask if the air conditioning can be slightly turned down, if it is extremely cold, always ask long before you are to stand and preach. If one has to preach in a church that is very cold, he or she should be sure that his or her attire will shield him or her in some fashion, and take care to immediately change clothes, if they heavily perspired, in spite of the cold conditions. For men and even some women, a hat is helpful after preaching, if you perspire; and, especially if you are preaching in a cold church, and when exiting the church to go outside to cold or cool weather.

When You Get to the Pulpit
Be sure to attend to the following:

- If possible, have the microphone adjusted before you stand. If you have to adjust it, do so quickly and without fanfare. If you are using a cordless microphone, be sure that it is not turned on before you stand to preach. Remember that most lavaliere microphones are wireless and, if turned on before you preach, they will pick up the slightest sounds. We've all heard the embarrassing stories about remarks that were made when speakers thought microphones were off.

- Before you stand to preach, remove all loose change from your pockets. This is always a good thing to do. If you tend to place your hands in your pockets as you preach (which is never good to do), rattling change can be extremely distracting.

- If you decide to pray as you stand, make it brief.

- Do not take a long time to introduce yourself. This was done previously by someone else and/or your brief bio most likely has been printed inside the order of worship. Just in case a church does not know you and does not have a bio for you, always take an extra one with you and extra business cards.

- It is appropriate for students who are home from school to thank the church for support and prayers. If you were once a member of the church where you are preaching, it is also appropriate to mention that fact.

- In your opening remarks, always acknowledge the pastor, even if he or she is not present. If a church is without a pastor when you preach, be certain to acknowledge the appropriate church officers and **have their names written down** before you stand. Also, depending upon your denomination and/or religious affiliation, it is appropriate to acknowledge church officials such as bishops, superintendents, elders, etc.— just be brief.

- If you have numerous family and friends who have come to hear you preach, it is best to have them stand as a group. Typically, only spouses, children, parents, and grandparents are individually acknowledged.

- Only sing a song before you preach, if there was not a sermonic selection sung before you stood and or if the energy in the church is particularly low and your singing prowess will help raise it. Other than this, save any singing until you have finished preaching. Conserve your voice for the preaching moment.

Reading Your Text(s)

Too often, preachers read the text(s) from which they will preach as if they are doing so to get it or them out of the way and get to the sermon. However, the reading of one's text is an important part of the preaching moment. Always read texts with energy. Verbally punctuate important words. Do not read too quickly or too slowly. Do not allow your voice to trail off when completing a scripture. If one of your texts is a narrative, read it as a brief story and pull in listeners, even at this point. Again, always read the Word of God with inspired energy and preach and conclude the same way.

After the Sermon

If you conclude with a prayer, make sure that it is connected to your behavioral aim and your sermon. Do not re-preach aspects of your sermon in your prayer. Also, immediately following a sermon, many Protestant churches have what is known as the "opening of the doors of the church," also known as "the moment of decision" or "the invitation." This is the time when people are invited to join a particular church. Do not open the doors of the church without permission from the pastor or the officials in charge of worship.

Be totally prepared to do the benediction, in case you are asked. If you do not know how to do a benediction, do not guess at it. There are examples from service books and there are many examples on the Web; use them. Just as the reading of scripture before the sermon is not to be taken for granted, neither is the benediction. Just before giving the benediction, it is customary for preachers to again thank the pastor and the congregation for extending an invitation to preach at the church.

As much as possible, rest your voice the day after you preach and drink large amounts of water (all week) for hydration. The throat is more sensitive than we understand. Overuse and failure to properly rest and hydrate the throat can cause long-lasting and extensive harm. More and more we hear stories of preachers who are having surgeries to remove vocal cord nodules and throat polyps. If you are new to preaching, begin practicing these habits now. This will greatly increase your vocal health in the future. If you are a more experienced preacher and are not in the habit of hydrating and resting your voice the day after you preach, you need to develop these habits, especially if you preach more than once each week.

Finally, if possible, review your sermon no later than the day after you preach it. If you want to improve your preaching, it must be assessed. If you have a CD or DVD of your message, listen to it. If not, at least write notes concerning what you believe you did well and what areas need work. Whenever you can, ask someone who preaches well to listen to the message and give you an honest assessment too. If you are new to preaching, you are likely still finding your preaching voice. The rule of thumb is that it takes ten to fifteen years to find your preaching voice, after one enters ministry and begins preaching regularly (twice each month). So, do not be alarmed if you are not yet comfortable with your preaching voice or style. Keep preaching, and falling in love with God and preaching, and you will gain what you need. If you are a seasoned preacher, you are assessing your preaching to see how you are maturing as a preacher. Remember, our preaching voices should change as we mature and our abilities should increase in all of the mechanics discussed in this study guide.

A SERMON TO SUM IT ALL UP

The successful use of this study guide depends on your repetition of the exercises. Good use of all of the lessons and exercises, I trust, are actualized by my example below, which pulls all of the lessons and exercises together in a sermon. The sermon is entitled, *A Tale of Two Boys*. The marginal notations relate the sermon back to the vehicles and instructions provided in the earlier chapters.

A TALE OF TWO BOYS

Behavioral Aim: To move hearers toward compassion for and use of practical, modern methods to help black boys.

Mark 9:14-29 (New Revised Standard Version)

14 When they came to the disciples, they saw a great crowd around them, and some scribes arguing with them. 15 When the whole crowd saw him, they were immediately overcome with awe, and they ran forward to greet him.

16 He asked them, 'What are you arguing about with them?' 17 Someone from the crowd answered him, 'Teacher, I brought you my son; he has a spirit that makes him unable to speak; 18 and whenever it seizes him, it dashes him down; and he foams and grinds his teeth and becomes rigid; and I asked your disciples to cast it out, but they could not do so.'

19 He answered them, 'You faithless generation, how much longer must I be among you? How much longer must I put up with you? Bring him to me.'

20 And they brought the boy to him. When the spirit saw him, immediately it threw the boy into convulsions, and he fell on the ground and rolled about, foaming at the mouth.

21 Jesus asked the father, 'How long has this been happening to him?' And he said, 'From childhood.

22 It has often cast him into the fire and into the water, to destroy him; but if you are able to do anything, have pity on us and help us.'

23 Jesus said to him, 'If you are able!—All things can be done for the one who believes.' 24 Immediately the father of the child cried out, 'I believe; help my unbelief!'

25 When Jesus saw that a crowd came running together, he rebuked the unclean spirit, saying to it, 'You spirit that keeps this boy from speaking and hearing, I command you, come out of him, and never enter him again!'

26 After crying out and convulsing him terribly, it came out, and the boy was like a corpse, so that most of them said, 'He is dead.' 27 But Jesus took him by the hand and lifted him up, and he was able to stand.

28 When he had entered the house, his disciples asked him privately, 'Why could we not cast it out?' 29 He said to them, 'This kind can come out only through prayer.'

Introduction

Do you believe the Black church still has power? Do you believe that, if you have faith the size of a tiny mustard seed, you can move mountains? Do you believe John 14, where it says: "He that believeth on me, the works that I do, shall ye do also; and **greater** works than these shall ye do"? I am glad you believe all of this. We'll come back to it later.

Move 1 Focus Topic Sentence: Our faith community has been tested and the text is a story about tested faith.

subⴟ a: African Americans come out of a tested and venerable faith community.

I believe so much is possible for us, because we come out of a faith community that has achieved so much against brutal, vicious, unjust odds. The African American faith community has phenomenal roots. Aren't you proud that we have such phenomenal faith community roots? Everyone wants to say that they come from good stock, good roots, a good background.

So, I'm proud that we come from a faith community that produced a Sojourner "got to tell it like it is" Truth. We produced E.K. Love, who pastored a 6,000-member church in the 1800s, helped start a college in Savannah, and helped form the National Baptist Convention. We produced Joseph Charles Price, called the "World's Orator" in 1881 by the London Times; he co-founded and was the first president of Livingston College in North Carolina, all by age 39, when he died of Bright's Disease.

> This section of the sermon names too many men and too few women.

And, we produced Charles H. Mason who formed the Church of God in Christ, and Charles Albert Tindley, who was the janitor of the church he later pastored and turned it into a 5,000-plus member mega church. And, during the Depression, the church opened a life-saving food pantry; and while he was doing all of that, he also wrote hymns we are still singing: "We'll Understand It Better By and By," "Stand by Me," and one of my favorites, "The Storm Is Passing Over," hallelu.

If I had time, I'd mention these preachers. We have phenomenal faith community roots. And don't ever forget all of the phenomenal lay people who have also been like celestial stars in guiding us toward our quest for freedom and dignity in this country.

> The preacher is aware that she has mentioned the preachers.

subⴟ b: Faith is tested as a man brings his son to Jesus.

What made those who are a part of our corpus, our lineage, the roots of our faith community, so strong, so venerated, so admirable? At least two things did it. One, they all knew that faith is not faith until it's tested; and, two, they were willing to tackle the big problems of their day, because of their faith.

That is what we have in our text, a story about faith being tested by a major problem—not your everyday run of the mill, gets on your last nerve, gives you a headache problem, but a major problem. The kind that knocks you on your knees and makes you wanna' pull out your weave problem.

Versions of this story are found in Matthew, Mark, and Luke. Mark's version is fleshed out more than the others. So, he will be our primary guide today. Here's how Mark tells the story. Mark says, "Jesus had been up on Mount Hebron (also called the Mount of Transfiguration) with three of the disciples (Peter, James, and John). They go up one day and come down the next. As they **descend** and reach the base of the mountain, Jesus and his boys see the other nine disciples. There's a crowd gathered around them. There is an argument going on. The Scribes (a group of **religious** leaders) are arguing with some of the disciples. Jesus asked, "What are you arguing about?" The scribes didn't answer. They were too busy arguing. The nine disciples Jesus left below, as he went up on the mountain, had just messed up by failing to fix the major problem at hand, so they didn't answer either.

Sooooo, [sic] a father spoke up. The father said, "Teacher, I brought my son, my only child here. He can't speak or hear and he has a demonic spirit that seizes him. It throws him down, he foams at the mouth, grinds his teeth, and becomes as stiff as a board. This evil spirit makes him go out of his mind, and at times it throws him into fires, and at other times into the river and he just cries a lot."

sub¶ c: The story of the boy who has D.D.D. is bad!

This son was in a bad way. I told you it was a major problem. His existence was **hell** on earth. The father in our story doesn't name his son's condition; he simply states what it makes the boy do. So, since he doesn't name it, can I tell you what I believe the boy had? I believe he had D.D.D.—**not** A.D.D. or A.D.H.D., but D.D.D. He was deaf (couldn't hear), dumb (couldn't talk), and he was demon-possessed. The demon possession presented (or exhibited itself) like a case of epilepsy.

Demons in scripture presented in various ways. Some made people cut themselves, like the biblical story of the man in the grave yard; or, there was the woman with a demon of infirmity; she was bent over for 18 years; and, there was the man who had so many demons (multiple personalities) he just said that they are legion, meaning thousands of them tormented him. So here, the demon presented with epilepsy. I believe this boy had D.D.D. He was deaf, dumb, and had a demon that presented with epilepsy.

The bible doesn't give the boy a name. So that we can see him better, so that I can help you really identify with this boy and see the depth of his story, let's call him Ben, which is a Jewish name, meaning son. Here lies Ben with D.D.D.

Ben's dad said, "When my son is seized by the demon, it tosses him into fires." So, in other words, here lies helpless Ben in front of the Scribes with D.D.D. and fresh burns all over his body, and all the scribes can do is argue with some of the disciples, as if Ben is either invisible or unimportant. They were probably arguing with the Disciples over who had the authority to cast out sins, since the belief at that time was that one had sinned, if one had any type of negative medical condition.

But, **meanwhile**, Ben is lying on the ground scarred, seizing, and suffering!

The words **descend** and **religious** are in bold here to remind me to give more inflection to these words. This is done throughout the sermon.

These actions by the son were acted out by a mime as I preached. The mime temporarily stopped after this section.

Sub-move c is unequal in length—much longer than the other sub-moves in this section of the sermon. Material should have been cut.

I used the word "dumb" because it is the word used until recent modern times to describe the boy's speech condition. It's not the best word to use.

Since the father is also unnamed, we can surmise that he is not a man of means. He was just a dad with a major problem. So, it's doubtful that he could afford to take his son to the trained physicians of that day, or it's possible he had already paid so many doctors he had run out of money.

The father could not afford a quid-pro-quo (pay a doctor, sow a seed, buy holy oil, and get healed) solution. He just needed some compassion and some grace. The father also couldn't take Ben to the temple because, in his condition, Ben would have been considered unclean. Still, the father was not willing to give up on his son. So, he brought Ben to Jesus.

So, Ben and his dad are **outside** and Ben's father answers Jesus, since no one else did. Ben Sr. said, "Teacher, I brought my son, I asked some of your disciples to cast out the demon, **but they couldn't do it.**"

This upset Jesus and he said, "You **faithless** generation. How much longer do I have to be among you and put up with you?" Then he said, "Bring the boy to me." Then, Jesus asked the father, "How long has the boy been like this?" The father said, "Since childhood." Then, the father said, "**If** you can do anything, have **compassion** on us."

In my sanctified imagination, I hear Jesus saying, "**If**? All things are possible for those who believe." In other words, Mr., you may not know what I can do, but I know. Don't confuse me with the Disciples. It's not on me. I know what I can do. It's on you! Can you believe? Can you muster enough faith about this **one thing** to believe it can be fixed? Sir, can you commit single-mindedly to this **one thing** long enough to believe it can be done? Sir, do you even have faith equal to the size of a small mustard seed, for your son's sake?"

Ben Sr. said, "Teacher, I believe, but help thou my unbelief." I believe that this is a noble statement made by a desperate dad. He's saying in so many words, "Jesus, I know who you are, so ain't no need of me frontin. But, let me be honest. I believe, but I've got some doubt too."

After Jesus sees the dad's need for compassion, the demon seizes the boy one last time. After that, Jesus heals the boy. The boy looked like a pale, ashy corpse at that point, so the crowd thought he was dead. So, Jesus had the boy to stand up so everyone could see that he was alive and fully healed.

> Here, the mime, who had remained stretched out on the floor, gets up.

And after all of this, when they left the scene and were alone with Jesus, the disciples asked, "Why couldn't we do that?" And Jesus told them that, for this type of case (a major problem), they needed to pray. In other words, they needed to be as spiritually fortified as possible.

Move 2 Focus Topic Sentence: The tale of Ben then, and the tale of our boy now.

sub¶ a. Allow me to introduce our boy.

> The mime slips out of his clothing worn for the first part of the sermon. He is now dressed in sagging pants, a t-shirt and a baseball cap turned backwards. He mimes until the end of the reading of the song lyrics.

Well, that's the end of the story. That was Ben and Ben Sr.'s story. **But this is a tale of two boys.** In 2012, another boy has a story. It's not Ben. It's Pookey. It's Bay-bay, or Deshawn, Malik, Andre, Jamal, or Darryl. It's not Ben Sr.'s boy; it's our boy, and our boy has a major problem too.

And, in 2012, parents are still bringing our boy to religious folks for healing. Some bring their boys on prayer lists and some even in person. Ben was brought by his dad. Our boy in 2012 would probably be brought by his mother, grandmother, or aunt. They, like Ben's father, assume that where you have religious folk gathered is where you bring a child who has a major problem.

Like Ben, our boy has also suffered from childhood. He was born in poverty to parents of no means. He was born into a system that does not provide support for black boys like him. That system is busy taking care of corporations that they think are people too. Our boy has a major problem.

Second, our boy also has D.D.D. One, he is dad-less (never knew his father). Two, he is dysfunctional (dropped out in the 5th grade and had a juvie record by age 11). And three, he too is demon-possessed.

His demon does not present as epilepsy; it presents as addiction, or violence, or hopelessness, or as illiteracy. Sometimes it presents as all of these at the same time. And this demon is now doing to our boy what was done to Ben: it throws him into fires and floods. It throws him into the fires that keep burning up his dreams and into floods that keep drowning his potential.

Our boy's theme song was written by Tupac Shakur. It's titled "Lord Knows." A verse of it says:

> *Every day is another death, with every breath, it's a constant threat. So watch your step. You could be next. If ya want to, who do you run to? My memories bring me misery, and life is hard in the ghetto, it's* **insanity**. *I can't breathe, got me thinkin'. What does hell got? Cause I don suffered so much I'm feelin'* **shell-shocked**.

I told you that this was a major problem!

subJ b: What happens when our boys go to church?

I told you that our boy's guardians assume that a place where religious folk gather is where they should take their boy. In the past, these places have been freedom centers, training grounds, birthing institutions for leadership, healing houses, and much more. We know what happened when Ben's dad brought him to the disciples.

What happens when today's parents bring boys before religious folk? As was the case with Ben, two things **usually** happen: one, the religious leaders (the deacons, the elders, and the sanctified saints) argue about what is allowed in their church. The second thing that **usually** happens is that the folk who should be able to heal our boys can't do it!

But, instead of asking like the disciples, "Why couldn't we do that?" these church folk say: "We don't know why these boys can't get their act together"—in other words, why can't they heal themselves? Or, the Church says: "Why didn't his mother raise him better?" Or, they say, "Why do folk wait until everything goes wrong before they come to the Church?" Do I have any witnesses? Do you know any church folk like that?

subJ c: We are perplexed and mainly embarrassed; transfiguration is needed.

The reason I talked about the scribes earlier is that in several ways they represent the broken 21st-century Church. This is a church stuck on the "letter of the law," meaning what used to work. They're stuck on what's not controversial, and they really just **don't** want certain types of folk in their church. The members of this church can quote scripture, they can do praise and worship, **but they can't heal anybody!**

This is a major problem. So, I believe it's time to transfigure the way we do church. The Disciples were no doubt perplexed and embarrassed. They had been trained and had some past spiritual accomplishments; they had been chosen and commissioned.

Aren't you embarrassed sometimes, too? Tell the truth. Aren't you perplexed too? Did you ever think it would come to this for **our** boys? Did you ever think that you would see so many of our boys on corners **every** day; on drugs, on dead-end streets? Did you ever think that some would talk the way they talk about black women? Did you ever think that it would be considered black macho by some to just father a child, even if you don't raise the child? Did you ever think that our boys (Pookey, Bay-bay, Deshawn, Malik, or Darryl) would celebrate project pimps, dime-store drug dealers, and thugs claiming jail time gives you street credit? We've got a major problem!

But, I wonder what did we really expect? Did we really think that boys, who were allowed to see too much too soon (violence and sex every day and everywhere), would be **alright**? Did we really think that boys whose parents were babies themselves would be **alright**? Did we really think that as black denominations kept spending huge sums of the community's money on and having conventions in white folk's hotels to do nothing for nobody, that our boys would be **alright**? Did we really think that the descendants of those who designed the capitalistic system of slavery would stop attacking black men, and our boys would be **alright**? Did we really think that as we took flight for the suburbs and sometimes moved our churches there too, that our boys would be **alright**?

We need a transfiguration of how we do ministry if we want to save our boys. Remember, this story comes after a transfiguration experience and that's what we need. You now know that we've got a major problem. But, I wouldn't come to just name the problem. Anybody can do that. I came to offer some solutions; and, they are all in the text.

Move 3 Focus Topic Sentence: There are ways to heal our boys.

sub¶ a: Go outside sometime.

The first solution to healing our boys is that we've got to go outside sometime. We have to go where they are. Notice that the boy in the text was outside. He wasn't in the temple. Guess where our boys are who are in trouble? They're outside. We can't do ministry just for those already inside the Church. Jesus could reach Ben because Jesus did not stay shut up in the temple; he spent a lot of time outside! Some youth leader is gonna get that on the way home.

Go outside sometime and get ready, because what you see outside may disturb some of your Bill Cosby-ish notions of respectability. The boys you meet will not dress like you or talk like you; but, they are still a part of you; and, deep down, they are no different than you. You may no longer know them—you may have outgrown them—you may be ashamed of them, but they still are our boys. All they really want is a good family, a decent job, and to be loved. Most just need some compassion and some grace.

Our boys speak a broken language, filled with anger, denial, distrust, and defeat. They speak in code. Their communication tools—how they talk, a hoodie, some tattoos, pants below the butt and underwear showin'—are their code for "will somebody see us." All of it —their "exaggerated utterances" and the clothes—is code for "Please notice us!"

Can I tell you a quick story? A group of young men moved into the complex, where I live. I was surprised to see them, because there were no really young adults in that part of the complex. I'd see them in the work-out area of the complex and I made it my business to speak to them and we'd talk about sports.

One day, I heard seismic-shaking level music that I could hear in my unit with my windows closed. So, I went **outside** to see who was violating the condo noise policy and it was the young men and a friend. I said, "Hello," and explained that I had not asked to be entertained by a concert via car. They turned the music off.

Then, I asked what they were celebrating so loudly, anyway. They laughed and that conversation went to my finding out more about them and them about me. And, as I was walking away, I said, "Someone is double-parked; that's another violation; and, you will get towed. Why don't you use my parking space. It's empty."

Now, when they see me coming, I'm greeted with a smile. They don't call me by my first name, or Auntie or Shortie. It's Ms. Simmons. The music is not turned up and they always want to know how I'm doing, and they take out my garbage. Now, in order for that relationship to begin, I had to go where? Outside. In order to heal our boys, we have to go where? Outside.

sub¶ b: Fight systems working collaboratively with others.

Let me move on. The second way to heal our boys is to attack some of the systems that are throwing them into fires and floods. The disciples were arguing with the scribes. The scribes were part of a system (they helped maintain the status quo). They were out to stop the work of the Disciples and Jesus. They could have cared less about a boy who needed healing. Also, the boy in our text was up against a government that collected taxes but did not provide him or his parents with health care. Somebody is gonna get that on the way home.

If you're old enough and informed enough, you know about all the systems that have conspired and continue to conspire to stop the progress of black males. Being the President does not even get you basic respect, if you are a black male. The systems that we must fight include: school systems, police departments, state legislatures, the media, the courts, corporations, politicians at every level, government agencies, denominations, and churches that have lost their way. Our boys don't know how to fight these systems—and they can't fight them alone. They just know that they keep gettin' thrown into hellish fires and never-ending floods.

One of the main systems that we need to fight now is the Prison Industrial Complex. There are more African Americans under correctional control today—in prison or jail, on probation or parole—than were enslaved in 1850, a decade **before the Civil War began**. And, do not kid yourself, this is not by accident. This is by design!

I am not a conspiracy theorist, but I do have common sense. You cannot have an ethnic group that is only 12% of the general population be almost 40% of the prison population, except by design. This is not about: "If they don't want to do the time, tell them not to do the crime." This is about too many boys being targeted, starting at third grade—over-charged, over-sentenced, and stigmatized for life.

Twenty-first century ministry requires transfiguration and collaboration to fight and transform these systems that prey on our boys. We don't need 500 churches in a city going it all alone. Every black church needs to partner with other churches and groups to fight the predatory systems of evil in our communities that are maiming and killing our boys.

Every black church needs to partner with other black churches to create at least one program that helps boys who are either on their way to, or, who have just come out of juvenile detention facilities—and girls too, but that's another sermon. In order to heal our boys, 21st-century black churches must begin to fight the systems that are preying on them.

We must be counter-cultural; not just relevant, but counter-cultural. Relevancy is fine. But, it's just the minimum standard. The Bible, in Acts 17, speaks of disciples who turned the world upside down. That's more than being relevant; it's counter-cultural. In the 21st century, we need churches that are counter-cultural.

I'm glad we now have churches with screens that also stream (that's the latest in technology). Glad we have praise and worship groups; I enjoy them. Glad we have churches with family life centers; we need them. But all of those things are just the starting point for a church—they show that you understand the need to be relevant. But the next step, the big step, "the **greater works shall you do**" step, is to use all of those things to be counter-cultural.

> This and the next paragraph were not necessary and made this already long sub-point longer.

What does this look like? Our foreparents on the list that I recited earlier, they were counter-cultural. It looks like them—it looks like what they did. They turned some things upside down and then right side up. Be more than relevant, be counter-cultural. Lyndon Baines Johnson was relevant in 1964 when we were trying to pass the Voting Rights Act. He was relevant, he was the President. But Martin Luther King Jr. was counter-cultural. He turned the world upside down and then right side up. P.W. Botha was the president of South Africa in 1983, when apartheid was at its height. He was relevant; he was the President. But Nelson Mandela, in a jail cell for 27 years, was counter-cultural. He turned South Africa upside down and then right side up. The scribes were relevant; they were the adjudicators of the law. But Jesus, who ignored their laws, when a boy was in trouble, he was counter-cultural. He turned the world upside down and then right side up!

sub¶ c: Have compassion and help parents who are in trouble.

Next, to heal our boys, we must have compassion on them and their parents. Positive parental involvement always helps boys who are in trouble. But, Ben's father had doubts. Ben's father needed help. He had been dealing with his son's condition, since his son was a child. We have parents and guardians who have been suffering with the demons that plague their children just as long. They believe God, but they have doubts too. Some of them are also just ill-equipped to be parents or guardians and are at their wits end.

We waste time, if we just preach down to these parents: "Raise your children right. Make your son pull up his pants. Know where your kids are at night. Set some boundaries for your kids. Teach your kids some manners. Make your son respect black women," etc. If preaching like this to the parents of our boys who are in trouble would do the trick, we wouldn't have any problems, because we've had a million of those sermons.

There are two problems with mainly using that approach. Number one, many of the parents at whom those messages are directed are not in the Church anyway. And two, many of the things that we know they should do, these parents do not know how to do. If they did, they would do them!

Jesus helped Ben's poor, doubting, desperate father. He only asked the man to have a little faith. He could have just said, "Sir, I really don't have time for anyone who doesn't have strong faith." But, Jesus had compassion on the boy and his father. They both needed help. Notice in the text that Ben's father said, "Have compassion on **us**." He didn't say just on my son.

As you come to the end of the sermon, you should have noticed by now that it lacks colors. This could have made it come alive even more.

Church, **our boys and their parents** who are in crisis need our compassion, coupled by solutions. So, instead of just another Bible study, why not hold parenting classes for parents you know are in trouble? Instead of just teaching the same ole Sunday school lesson, "Pharaoh got drowned in the Red Sea," why not teach Sunday school students to be lifeguards, so they can help some drowning parents or at least get them to someone who can. Show some compassion.

Instead of just another revival every year to fill out the church calendar, why not hold a revival on purpose—a revival, where churches go get lost parents and boys; and, in partnership with other groups that can help, invite them to church for a purpose.

Do this type of transfigured ministry so that after we have finished praise and worship and jumpin' and shoutin', someboddddddddddy [sic] **has been healed**! We can show parents where they have gone wrong, after we show them some compassion.

Then, as Jesus is about to heal Ben, the scripture says that the demon seized Ben one last time. So, when you begin working with our boys, expect the devil to take one last stand, so you'll need compassion that is patient too. The devil never gives up easily, especially when he has had a hold of someone since childhood. When vicious and deadly habits take root for a long time, they are hard to cure. So, expect that some boys may backslide, because the devil does not go down without a fight.

sub¶ d: We must pray to heal our boys.

The next thing that will heal our boys is prayer. Jesus said, this type of solution (the solution for a major problem) requires prayer. The other solutions I've given you are **suggested** by the text, but prayer is **specifically recommended by Jesus** in the text.

Surely, the disciples had prayed before. But, when Jesus said this type of problem requires prayer, what he meant was that the hard cases (the boys on meth cases, the boys with guns cases, the cases most folk have given up on), these cases require **special** preparation. They require that you be prayed up—not do give-it-a-shot-because-you're-in-a-spot prayer.

Move 3 of the sermon is unbalanced and has too many sub-moves. One should have been removed.

Let me tell you a last, quick story. A group of young preachers were thrilled to visit the church of the master preacher, Charles Spurgeon. He had the largest church in London at the time and one of the largest in the world. When they arrived at the church, a man met them at the door and asked if they wanted to see the church's heating system. The young preachers were confused. Who would want to see a church's dirty heating system? But, they did not want to be rude, so they followed the man downstairs. When they got downstairs, the man opened a door, and there they saw 700 saints bowed in prayer. This, the man said, is our heating system. **Prayer is still the Church's heating system!**

We will not heal our boys, as long as we will show up in droves for our favorite sporting event, movies, or Kirk Franklin, Mary Mary, and Shirley Caesar concerts, **but** will not show up for prayer meeting. The difficult work **can't be done** without continuous prayer and sometimes fasting.

I heard Rev. A.C. Dixon say, "When we rely upon organizations we get what organizations can do. When we rely upon education, we get what education can do. When we rely upon ourselves, we get what we can do. And all of these have their place. But when we rely upon prayer, we get what God can do!" So, let's start praying and let's start working. We've got to start and keep at it.

In the text, the community thought Ben was dead the last time the demon jumped on him. But he wasn't dead, he just **looked** like it. Many of us think our boys are dead too. But they are not; it just **looks** like it. But, no matter how bad they look, join me in vowing that we won't ever give up on them.

Celebration Focus Topic Sentence: We can save our boys because of what is said in John 14.

sub¶ a: Topic Sentence: We won't give up on our boys and we can do this.

<table>
<tr>
<td>From this point, through the conclusion of the celebration, the mime is active.</td>
<td>

- We won't give up on Malik, the high stakes hustler. He could be a future pastor. Remember, Zacchaeus was first a tax collector who stole from the poor.

- We won't give up on Pookey, the drug dealer. He could be the future chair of a deacon board. Remember, the Apostle Peter acted like a thug, carried a knife, and used it.

- We won't give up on Bay-bay, the gang leader. He could be the future chair of your Trustee board. Remember, the Apostle Paul was first a co-conspirator to murder.

</td>
</tr>
</table>

We won't give up on our boys; we can do this! We've tackled bigger problems than this. We've been counted out before. We've fought against meaner systems before. Remember slavery, Reconstruction, Deconstruction, Jim Crow, and Jane Crow?

We can do this. Jesus said: "Greater things will you do if you believe." Since Jesus said this, that means that on top of everything that I named that will heal our boys, we have a secret weapon. Yeah, we've got a secret weapon. Well, it's only a secret to those who haven't tried the weapon. Our secret weapon is a who, not a what. **Do you know who he is?** Jesus is our secret weapon! Jesus is there to help us do whatever we need to do.

sub¶ b: Topic Sentence: We are not failures and great things will happen as we save our boys.

The disciples failed in our text. They suffered embarrassment that time. They were perplexed that time. The disciples are just like us. We are fallible; we are flawed, but, we are not failures. We may fail sometimes, but we are not failures. After the disciples failed that time, Jesus still left the Church in their hands.

And by and by, after a while, they were accused of turning the world upside down. That means that there is hope for you and me. Thanks be to God for our secret weapon. When the disciples missed it, they despaired. But, why despair when such a mighty Savior is willing to help us? "Greater works shall you do if you believe on him."

I wish I had about 10 people who would help me say greater! I'm claiming it today for this church. You're gonna save some boys. Greater! More educated boys—greater! Boys off the corner—greater! Boys putting down guns—greater! Boys off drugs—greater! Boys who are good dads—greater! Boys helping you turn this city upside down. Upside down. Upside down! Upside down, upside down, and then right side up. Right side up. Right side up. Right side up. Do I have a witness? Turn it how? **Upside down!** Turn it how? **Upside down!** And then, right side up. Right side up. Right side up!

At the last paragraph of the celebration, the mime threw down a fake gun and a fake syringe. He took off his hat and pulled up his pants. He concluded by doing hand and arm motions to symbolize the phrase upside down and then the phrase right side up. One of the arm motions was done swiftly to form the shape of a cross.

NOTES

NOTES

NOTES

NOTES

NOTES

NOTES

NOTES

NOTES

NOTES

NOTES

NOTES